THE GREAT AWAKENING

Volume - III

A series of superbly informative and prophetic messages,
downloaded and transcribed originally as newsletters by

Sister Thedra

These precious messages are reprinted herein.

ISBN: 978-1-7363418-7-2

Contents

Mission Statement

Give the truth to the world. Let it be received where it will. Many will read the messages. Some will accept the truth, others will read through curiosity, a few will ridicule. Yet to all is the truth given, and to all remains the power of choice.

The hope of the world in these times is in spiritualizing all forms of activity---promoting understanding through love and service. These must be the watchwords if the world is to come into lasting peace. We are trying to influence a world that is going astray and could cause undreamed of suffering. We are trying to overcome the thought of materialists and to bring a spiritual outlook into the earthly life. We need the help of all on earth who can think in spiritual terms. The great battle to be fought now is between the spiritual and the material, between idealism and carnalism. You can help by spreading the word---we are asking that you help because the battle may be long and the victory far away.

Halls of Light is not allied with any sect, denomination, political entity, organization, neither endorses nor opposes any cause. There are no dues for membership. Halls of Light is self-supporting through its own voluntary contributions. Halls of Light has but one purpose: to help through encouragement and understanding...

To contact the publishers or to obtain copies of our other books, please contact us at email: goldtown11@gmail.com

Esu Jesus Sananda

This reproduction is from an actual photograph taken on June 1st, 1961, in Chichen Itza, Yucatan, by one of thirty archaeologists working in the area at the time. Sananda appeared in visible, tangible body and permitted His photograph to be taken.

THE TEMPLE OF SANANDA & SANAT KUMARA

Warriors for The Mighty Cause

Hear ye! Hear ye that which I say -- For it is now come - when the Word shall go forth - which shall call all men to the front ---

I say ALL men shall be called to go forth - that this day might bring forth fruit of a new kind---

I too say - that this day shall be as NONE OTHER -- For it is the day for which they have waited -- Now they shall go forth as warriors anew -- Warriors for the Mighty Cause - for the TRUTH - LIGHT and JUSTICE -- These shall stand as upon the ROCK -- They shall not be moved -- For it is come when the CALL hast gone out: "Surrender up thineself and give unto Me thine WHOLE HEART - THINE WILL - THINE LIFE - for it is MINE ---

I have given or MINESELF that ye have LIFE ---

So be it I AM the "SOL" - I AM HE which hast ENSOULED thee with MINE BEING - and I ask of THEE - be ye as ONE with ME - and ye shall go forward into BATTLE - with thine WHOLE ARMOR OF LIGHT - which none shall take from thee ---

I say - ye shall hold high the LAMP of TRUTH and JUSTICE - and no man shall put thee down - or tread upon thee -- I say: "Stand ye high among men - and resist them not - for they are but the ones which shall go down into defeat ---

1

For NO man shall stand against the Warriors of LIGHT --- Hear ye Mine Words - for I have sent forth a FIAT which shall protect them which carry the BANNER OF TRUTH and JUSTICE ---

So be it I speak unto thee as thine Father Eternal –

Such AM I --.

And I AM thine Father

Solen Aum Solen

Recorded by Sister 'Thedra of the Emerald Cross

No Thorns for Thine Brow

Holy - Holy is the Name of Solen Aum Solen – Peace be unto thee this day -- For I say unto thee - the time is now come when the hour hast struck - when ye shall SEE and KNOW the POWER of the "WORD" -- Holy - Holy is THE WORD" - See the power thereof - and use it for the GLORY of THE FATHER which hast sent ME ---

See ye the WORD made manifest - and create ye no thorns for thine brow -- I say unto thee: "Create No thorns for thine brow" -- So be it I come that there be LIGHT -- SO LET IT BE ---

I AM Sananda

Recorded by Sister Thedra of the Emerald Cross

2

Mis-Interpretation of The Holy Writ

Beloved of Mine Being -- Hast it not been said that this is the time of gathering in? -- And it is so -- It is given unto Me to be one of the Great and Mighty Council - and I know wherein they are -- And it is given unto Us of The Council to be as Ones prepared to go forth that this day be the beginning of a New Order-- I say: "That this day be the beginning of a NEW ORDER"--

And it shall be as none "man" hast known - for it shall be the Order of the New Day - wherein ALL men shall sit down at the Council table as Brothers - and they shall BE as Brothers of ONE ORDER - wherein they shall LOVE one another - and be as the One which has the peace which surpasses all that which man hast ever known ---

For --

I say unto thee: the New Day shall bring great changes in the complexion of the affairs of men -- For there shall be Great Ones raised up amongst them - which shall KNOW the LAW -- And they shall be within the Law - to govern the affairs of the Government -- And for this shall they be given GREAT POWER -- For they shall be sent - even as I Am sent - that the Plan be fulfilled - that the day bring forth the fulfillment of the Scriptures ---

I say unto them - which hast fortuned unto themself the part of interpreting the Scriptures: "Be ye not so sure that thou art so wise" - for thou hast blundered mightily in thine interpretation of the records handed down through the ages past -- Thou hast changed the Words to suit thine own way - thine own went -- I say - as it hast

suited man - he hast put upon the Sacred Writ his interpretation --
He hast bled white the crimson rose -- He hast taken from the salt
its savor -- And if the salt hast lost its savor wherein shall it be salt?
-- Such is Mine preachment for this hour -- And I Am want to speak
on this subject again and again -- So be it I shall -- For this do ye
now wait --

I bless thee with Mine Presence -

with Mine Being --

I AM Sanat Kumara

Recorded by Sister Thedra of the Emerald Cross

These Are The Adversaries

Beloved of Mine Being -- Say unto them this day that it is NOW
come when they shall turn from their old way - in which they have
gone - and they shall NOW turn their face homeward -- For the
"END TIME" is now come when they shall no more wander: upon
the Earth as ones in bondage - THE WAY" is opened for their return
-- Yet they shall choose their way -- And it is given unto Me to see
them following after 'Strange gods" - while I Am crying unto them
"Come - follow ye ME" -- They hear not Mine cries - yet they follow
blindly the ones which come in Mine Name - declaring falsely. that
they are from afar - that they are THE deliverers!!

I say unto them: These are the false ones which cry out -- They
are sent for the purpose of distracting thee from the TRUTH/ from
the Light -- They say unto thee - LOOK there - look afar - and behold
what is doing there -- While thou hast held within thine OWN

4

HAND - the key to thine own salvation/ thine own preparation for the Greater Part ----

These are the enemies of the Truth -- These are the adversaries -- These are the false ones - and I shall point them out -- And they shall be known for that which they are -- For Justice shall prevail -- -

I say unto thee - be ye about thine own affairs - that of preparing thineself for the Greater learning - the fulfilling of THE LAW -- Live ye this Day - and be ye not fearful for thine life - for thine life is not of a Moment -- It is Eternal - and Great is The Work of The Almighty Father which hast sent ME --

I say unto thee - place thine hand on Mine - and I shall lead thee out of bondage ---

Yet none shall bring thee against thine will --

So be it I Am the One sent that there

Be Light -- I speak unto thee as

One or The Mighty Council - for I AM

The Head of the Council which IS

and shall BE - Worlds without end --

I AM Sananda

Recorded by Sister Thedra of the Emerald Cross

5

They Ask: "Where is He?"

Beloved Ones -- This day let it be known that I the Lord thy God hast come - come unto thee - come that ye be made glad - come that ye be prepared to return unto the Father with Me -- It behooves Me to say unto them which seek the Light - Which I AM - that they shall not be denied -- Yet I too say - that they shall be prepared to receive Me and of Me -- And it is clearly and wisely stated that a "As they are prepared - so shall they receive" - it is the LAW -- I tell thee it is now come when they shall cry out for Light - and I shall hear their cries - and they shall be given as they are prepared to receive -- It is said many times - yet they weary of Mine Word - Mine Counseling - and they look for strange gods and miracles -- For this have they been fortuned great sorrow ---

They are now asking - Where is He which cometh? Where IS HE? - The Man of many miracles? -- They want to see the marks upon the body -- They ask for proof!! -- Yea - Mine beloved - I say unto thee - they ask that they put their fingers into the wounds -- Yet I say - never again shall I bare Mine wounds unto them - for they are no more - no more do I carry Mine marks upon Mine body -- For Mine is not of Earth - Mine is the body of Light substance -- Yet I can take upon Mineself the flesh - as it suits Mine purpose -- I Am the Master of the Elements - and I know the way of the Elements - and too I know the weakness of flesh ---

I say unto thee there is Power in THE WORD - and I KNOW that Power - and I use it wisely that Mine Father be Glorified -- So let it Be ----

Be ye blest this day --

6

I have spoken that it be so --

So let it BE --I AM Sananda

Recorded by Sister Thedra of the Emerald Cross

"Patience" - "Sports"

Beloved Ones -- This day let Us speak of patience -- I say unto thee: - It is not afar off when ALL knees shall bend - and every head shall be bowed ---

Yet - - it is given unto "Man" to be a rebellious lot -- It is not the way of "man" to humble himself before the Great and Mighty Power - Which IS the CAUSE of his BEING ---

He is wont to forget ye Source of his Being -- He is prone to forgetfulness ---

Yet - he shall be brought to remembrance - he shall be caused to remember ---

Now - it is the way of the Initiate to stand be in readiness to assist him. When he has prepared himself to receive the assistance of the "Initiate"---

The "Initiate" is One which knows the Way back unto <u>his</u> place of abode - from whence he hast gone out -- He hast earned his "passport" into the "Holy of Holies"-- He hast been as one prepared to render assistance anywhere at any time - to anyone so prepared to receive such assistance -- <u>For he knows the LAW - and he does not violate it</u> ---

He walks with circumspection and prudence - wearies not of his waiting! -- He is at ALL times mindful of his part - which is part of the "Great and Grand Plan" -- And he is in no way of a mind to betray himself or his trust ---

He is want to become one with the Mighty Plan - for he knows the Way of the Initiate - and he is at all times concerned with the Greater Part -- Trivialities are none of his fortune - for he hast the knowledge of all that it fortunes unto man ---

He gives not of himself unto <u>gaming</u> -- He hast seen the results thereof -- The time is now come when many shall give themself over to such as the so-called "Sports" - and they shall devote their energies unto this as an occupation -- <u>For their sake let it be said that it is the way of the DRAGON - "Drag-ON" - for it is the long way 'round!</u> ---

I say: it is the poor fortune of man - for I say unto him: "there are more profitable things to occupy thine time - and consume thine energy -- So be it thine Guardians simply wait - that ye might learn well thine lessons -- And it shall behoove the young men to turn to the plowshares - and be as the plowmen -- For I say - it is now come when the fields shall be deserted - and they shall yield up no harvest -- And the wind shall blow - and the dust shall cover the land - and the water shall be as the dirt -- Wherein is it said that there shall be great suffering? -- Yet there shall come a season when the rains shall come - and the waters shall cover the land and the men shall be no more seen upon the land -- And they shall know that the "End time" is upon them -- So be it that I have spoken wisely and prudently - that they might be as ones alert - and turn unto the ways of the "knowing ones" - and be as one with them - that these things might not need be -- For it is the way of mankind to hasten the coming events by his own deeds -- The deeds and thoughts are as the sprouts upon which shall grow the thorns - which shall tear his own flesh - yea even unto the very bone! ---

I speak that they might be spared -- I say unto thee: Be ye no part of their wonton ways -- Be ye no part of their willfulness -- Be ye not fearful - for I Am come that ye might come to know the Way of the Initiate -- That ye might walk int the way in which I have gone ---

I say unto THEE: "Come - FOLLOW YE ME - and I shall lead thee out before the day of Great Suffering" -

I AM the Lord thy God sent

that ye might KNOW

even as I KNOW -

So be it I AM Sananda

Recorded by Sister Thedra of the Emerald Cross

The Glad Cry!

Beloved of Mine Being -- Be ye blest to receive Me this day - for I give of Mineself that ye might be blest -- Now it is come when there shall be a GLAD CRY go forth - and it shall reverberate around the Earth!! -- I say it shall reverberate around the Earth!! ---

And there shall be great rejoicing - and many shall fall upon their knees in gratitude – While others shall quickly forget that which hast been unto them great blessing -- They shall turn unto their plowing - and sowing - and unto their places of merry-making in forgetfulness ---

For this is the way of man -- Let it be said that there shall be great Light shed upon the peoples of the Earth - and great shall be their revelations - for it is NOW come when they which seek the Light shall find it - for IT SHALL NOT BE HIDDEN -- I speak unto thee that they might have this Mine Word - that "they" might bear witness of that which I say unto thee ---

So be it I AM Sananda

Recorded by Sister Thedra of the Emerald Cross

Sanandas Blessing

Behold this day the Work which I - the Lord God shall do -- Behold the Way of The Lord thy God - and be ye blest -- Walk ye in the way of the Lord - and know ye that it is the Way of Light - The Light Which "NEVER FAILS" -- I say unto thee - be ye blest this day -- For this do I speak unto thee ---

Let thine hand be Mine hand - thine words Mine Words - and let thine time be Mine time - and I shall abide with thee ---

So be it - I give of Mineself that ye be blest

So let it be I AM Sananda

Recorded by Sister Thedra of the Emerald Cross

Mine Son -Solen Aum Solen

O - Holy art Thou Mine Son - Mine Son which I have named Sananda - by Divine right. He Mine Son cometh unto Me as Mine First Born. I give unto Him the Name from the beginning of His sojourn upon the planet Earth - I give it Him in remembrance.

I speak of Mine son as the "First Born" - for is He not?

I say unto thee: He, Mine Son, the One I have given the Name Sananda, hast now come unto Me on thine behalf, that He might have greater - yet greater concourse with thee; that ye might be as ones prepared to enter into HIS place of abode. <u>I ask of thee nothing save obedience unto the Law; and walk ye after Him</u>. Him which I have sent unto thee - that ye might return unto Me with Him, Mine Son Sananda.

I speak unto thee in His Presence, that ye might bear witness of Mine Word. I tell thee as He would, that thou art the ones called out from amongst them; that the Order of Melchezedek be fortuned thine service, which is as none other at this time. For this have I called thee, and thou hast answered: "Here am I". I have not denied thee; I have not cut thee off from Mineself.

I bid thee enter into the Holy of Holies, and partake of Mine Substance, O Holy ones of Israel. <u>Walk ye after him, Mine Son Sananda, and pass into the Inner Temple as ones purified and justified</u>.

I AM Solen Aum Solen

Recorded by Sister Thedra of the Emerald Cross

11

Strange Gods – Counseling with the Dead

Behold in ME the Light -- Behold in ME the WAY - and give unto Me credit for Knowing that which I say unto thee - for I Am come that ye too - know even as I KNOW -- So let it be ---

Rest thine head upon Mins breast and give ye a gladsome prayer that it is now come when ye shall walk with Me - and ye shall know Me AS I AM - and none shall deceive thee -- I say unto thee NONE shall deceive thee - for it is given unto thee to KNOW ME - and none other shall be as I AM -- Yet many shall mimic Me - and many shall come declaring that they come in Mine Name -- Yet I say unto thee - I Am come unto thee that ye might KNOW THE TRUE FROM THE FALSE -- So let them which ask of the dead have their gods and their guides -- Yet ye shall not counsel with the dead - or ask of strange gods miracles -- So be it I Am sufficient unto ALL thine NEEDS --

I Am come that ye be lifted up --

So Be It - I AM Sananda

Recorded by Sister Thedra of the Emerald Cross

Is All Well with Thee?

Beloved Ones; - Who amongst thee is qualified to be unto Me Sibor? Who amongst thee is prepared to lift thee up? Who amongst thee is prepared to give unto thee passport into the place of Mine Abode? Who amongst thee has qualified for the part which is Mine by Divine Right?

I say unto thee: I AM the "Door thru which ye enter into the Inner Temple". I say unto thee: I am come that ye be lifted up. So be it that I come solely for Mine Love for thee, for it is Love which hast sent Me forth as One qualified for the part which is MINE.

So be it that I am qualified to say unto thee: "Come follow ye ME, and I shall lead thee into the place wherein MINE FATHER ABIDES". So be it that He hast SENT ME that it BE, and no man shall deny Me Mine inheritance, for it is MINE by DIVINE RIGHT. And at no time shall Mine inheritance be pilfered or dissipated, for it is given unto Me to be true unto Mineself and Mine trust. So all is well with Me - canst thou say as much? Let it be so; for this do I speak unto thee thusly, that it BE SO.

While I say: There are many which know Me not, they shall come to know ere they pass the portal of Light into the Inner Temple. Hold ye no ILLUSIONS, for I speak unto thee that ye know the true from the false; so be it that I am come that ye KNOW.

So be it that there are many, which shall have a long and troubled sleep ere they awaken; yet it is given unto the SLEEPER to awaken in due season,

For this do I now cry out; "AWAKEN! AWAKEN!" and all the Nations SHALL hear in due season.

While the peoples of the Earth shall spill blood of their brothers, and they shall over-run the lands (the black hordes), and they shall stamp the soil upon which they tread with their signs; they shall call themself "Righteous", and call their wars "Holy". Holy? I ask, holy? Wherein have they loved their fellowmen? Wherein have they

13

qualified themself to sit in judgment? Wherein have they been ordained of ME, the Lord of Lords, the Host of Hosts, the Lord God, sent that there BE LIGHT? I say unto thee: They desecrate the Earth! They pillage the poor! They are wont to give heed unto Mine Word, the LAW which is that by which they shall attain unto the Greater Part (their Eternal Freedom). I say unto them: Be ye not deceived, for NO MAN enters into the Inner Temple save by ME.

So be it I AM THE HOST OF HOSTS, LORD OF LORDS, SIBOR OF SIBORS, THE LORD GOD, Sent of Mine Father, which hast given of Himself that ye might have Everlasting Life. So let it BE.

I AM Sananda

The Light Which Faileth Not

Beloved Ones -- While it is yet time - let it be understood that there is a mighty force abroad within the land - and it is such as would consume them which have not the comprehension of the Light which IS - which has always been - and always shall BE ---

Yet these which have set this force into action know not the Light - for they are of the darkness - and the Light is not within them ---

They serve the darkness - they generate the darkness and for that matter they fear the Light -- They fear that which they do NOT KNOW! ---

For (because) they are aware of the soil upon which they put their feet - they know that they have footing upon the Earth - while

14

they desecrate it by the willful way which is theirs - by choice -- I say they have free will to choose which way they go - yet they have sold their birthright for a poor penny - and they have given over their freedom unto them which would hold them bound in darkness -- I say unto them: ARISE! - Claim thine Sonship - and be ye as ones responsible for thine own self - and know ye that there is Light - The Light <u>which</u> <u>faileth</u> <u>not</u> -- So be it that I AM the Light I AM the WAY --

Come ye - follow ye ME --

Walk ye in the Light --

And be ye as One free

from all bondage - forever --

I AM the Lord thy God -

Sananda

Recorded by Sister Thedra of the Emerald Cross

The First Law – Way of The Initiate

For this day, let us consider the 'WORD"; and it is for the GOOD of ALL that we take unto ourself this consideration.

When "The WORD" goes out of Mine mouth, it is designed to benefit ALL beings everywhere! and for this is the WORD sent forth. Yet we <u>know</u> that all shall not receive it unto themself, for all are not as yet prepared to drink of MINE CUP!

They have not prepared themself for to receive ME or of ME!

I say unto them: "AWAKEN! Arise and prepare thineself that I might come in and sup with thee".

Yet they weary of Mine WORDS; they hear not that which I say. They ask not for Mine way; they choose the "easy" way EASY? I ask of them, Easy? wherein hast the way of bondage been easy? I ask of them obedience unto the law, while they tarry in the streets of despair. They sing the song of the desolate the forlorn, the hopeless, they despair of their lot, yet they have not the strength of CHARACTER to walk in the way which I go.

They despair of the way in which I lead them; I say unto them: "Come! follow ye Me", and they tire of the upward climb - of the preparations; yet they grovel within the places of darkness for a poor penny, a pittance indeed!!

While I say unto them: "'Let them which have a mind COME, take up Mine Cross and follow", they weary of the discipline which it entails, <u>for I say unto them: The way of the Initiate is thru self-dedication and discipline, and none attain unto the heights until they have learned WELL, discipline - for it is the FIRST LAW, that of OBEDIENCE UNTO THE LAW</u>!

For the LAW never fails - It is IMPARTIAL and exact in its action, and none invalidate it.

Such is Mine Word this day. Let it be given unto them which have a mind to receive it.

So be it Mine hand is upon thee - I bless thee, that <u>they</u> be blest. So let it BE.

I AM Sananda

Recorded by Sister Thedra of the Emerald Cross

The Order of Melchezedeck

Beloved Ones -- Mine hand is upon thee this day - and I give unto thee this Word that ALL be blest thereby -- It is said that the Order of Melchezedeck is not of the Earth - it is so -- And it is now come when the Earth shall become a greater part of the Order -- For it is through and by the Order - which is the Mighty Council - that this Great Work of purifying the Earth and making it a habitable place for the Sons of God -- It hast been said; "The Sons of God shall inherit the Earth" - it is so -- Yet She shall be purged - cleansed - and She shall be as One made new -- For that matter - She too shall come into Her own - through and by the efforts of the MIGHTY COUNCIL - and it is given unto Her now - to be going through great change and great stress ---

<u>We of the Council work without ceasing - that the Earth and the Children thereof be lifted up</u> -- And we are not limited unto the Earth in our activity -- Ours is a Work of Love - of long duration - and Infinite in scope -- So be it ye shall come to know the fullness of Our activity - the FULLNESS of which no man knows - until he has won his freedom from bondage---

I speak unto thee of The Order of Melchezedeck that ye might come to know thine oneness with it -- That thou art One with It - of

It -- And for this have I spoken unto thee of this/ in this manner - for it behooves Me to give unto thee this Word at this time - for I see the wisdom thereof - and for this shall ye be blest ---

I AM the Lord thy God

Sananda

Recorded by Sister Thedra of the Emerald Cross

The End is in Sight

Behold the hand of God -- SEE it move - and know ye that it moves in ways beyond the comprehension of men -- For it is the POWER of the ALMIGHTY GOD - THE FATHER Which shall sweep away all the unsightly - unholy places - and that which hast accumulated therein -- I say it is THE POWER OF THE ALMIGHTY GOD Which shall cleanse the Earth and bring Her into the place of Her new berth -- So be it that it shall be accomplished - and She shall be spared!

I say She shall be spared!! -- So be it according unto the LAW - --

I Am come that the LAW be fulfilled - that the Scriptures be fulfilled -- And at no time shall I deny Mine Love - Mine Service unto the Earth - or the Children thereof -- Yet it is given unto Me to know the sorrow and the groaning of these which deny Me -- And as for the Earth - She hast cried long for deliverance - and She hast fulfilled Her part of the Plan -- She hast been the resting place of the SLEEPERS - and the footstool of the laggards -- Now She shall throw them off and be as one free of Her burden - So be it I speak

18

unto thee of that which is NOW IN PROGRESS -- So be it that the lands of the Earth shall be overrun with the "black hordes" before the Earth is delivered out -- Yet I say unto thee - the END IS IN SIGHT! - and I KNOW -- So let it BE ---

For it shall end in a Great Victory for the Earth - which hast received thee unto Herself - as the place wherein thou hast learned many lessons - and wherein thine Victory is won ---

So be it I speak unto thee -

So let it be for the good of all --

I AM Sananda

Recorded by Sister Thedra of the Emerald Cross

... These Mine Children

Beloved of Mine Being -- Behold in these Mine Children the Light -- See in them the Light -- Know ye that these Mine Children are in the WAY with Me ---

I say they are in the WAY with Me -- For this have they come - - Now ye shall be as one blest to receive them ---

Wait upon Me -- The Father which hast sent Me - shall give unto thee thine part - which is kept for thee -- Hold out thine hand and I shall place within it Mine - and I shall give unto thee a part unknown unto thee - and no man shall pilfer it - or put it within HIS pocket -- So be it I bless thee this day --

I AM Sanat Kumara

19

Recorded by Sister Thedra of the Emerald Cross

The Lesser Brothers

Mine Children -- Behold ME in ALL things -- See ye the Life of MINE BEING - I have endowed unto ALL Mine Creation ---

I have created WISELY - and I have given unto Mine Creation power to create like unto Its kind -- Yet I have set man apart - as a part separate from all other -- <u>For I have endowed unto him FREE WILL – and a part which hast not been given unto the lesser of Mine Creation</u> ---

This Gift sets him apart and above his lesser brothers -- Yet I say unto thee - the lesser brothers are none-the-less dear unto Me -- For they too shall find their rightful place wherein they shall know Peace -- For they too shall come into their own realm wherein they shall bring forth Greater manifestation - and wherein they shall be given a new part -- They shall come to have <u>new</u> forms of a finer density - of greater light density -- And they shall bring forth Greater intelligent beings - creatures of <u>great</u> intelligence such as man hast not seen -- And man shall wonder at these creatures of great beauty and intelligence -- Yet it is given unto man to be the Guardian of these lesser brothers - the Guardians which have the fortune to be born with the precious - precious gift of FREE WILL -- So be it thou art entrusted with these creatures - which too have their place -- So be it thou art no less for being their Guardians - while they too shall be lifted up -- Theirs is no small part - for they too are of the Plan - within the GREAT PLAN –

So be it I have spoken and thou hast heard ME

20

I AM - thine Father Solen Aum Solen

Christmas - 1975

Sori Sori - I say unto thee: There are none so foolish as the one which thinks himself wise - none so sad as the one which betrays himself.

Now it is come when the world reels and rocks; when the child of the Earth stands on the brink or destruction. Yet he plays his merry tune, and sings his songs of the idiot's delight. He feels no responsibility for the terrors which hound him; the terrors by night shall increase by day, and he shall be devoured by his fears and anxiety - for he hast created within him the monster which shall swallow him up.

The child of Earth which hast betrayed himself and his trust, shall be unto himself traitor; he shall be his own tormentor; his own accuser and his own judge. While I say, Justice shall reign supreme, I too say that the way of the transgressor is hard, and he shall know remorse and pity - for it is now come when the traitor shall know that he has betrayed himself, and his trust.

I say unto him, there shall be a place provided for him, where he shall wait for the fulfilling of the law; wherein he shall atone for all the misused energy and all the hypocrisy; all the hatred and the transgressions.

By the WORD shall he be brot to his fullness, his maturity, wherein he shall be responsible for his deeds; and he shall be as one prepared to enter into the realms of Light.

The Word hast gone out, and many a messenger have I sent that they might know the law, and be prepared for the realm of light. Wherein have they heard and headed the Word?

I say they have persecuted, ridiculed, slandered, the ones sent that they be brot out before the day of sorrow. So let them ask of Me the Light, and I shall send One unto them, which shall direct and teach them - enlighten them; and they shall be comforted in the time of suffering. So be it and Selah.

Say unto them, that there shall be a great wave of Light which shall flood the Earth; and all which are not one with it shall fall before it, for none which are not with it shall stand before it.

So be it that they shall be as ones blinded by it, for I say it shall be as nothing seen before - for the Light shall consume the darkness.

Now I say unto all: Look unto the Light for thy Salvation, and ye shall not perish. So be it I am come that ALL have Light more abundantly, and the way is made strait. I now call unto ALL: Look! Listen! See and hear that which the Spirit sayeth, and no harm shall he thine. So be it and Selah.

Recorded by Sister Thedra

Christmas - 1976

Sori Sori -- This hour I would say unto all which ask the Light, that I AM COME. At this hour I speak unto all which have ears to hear.

Be ye aware of the Light which I AM - I am come of The Light; I am within It, and of It, for I AM that I AM. I bargain not for man's souls, for I compromise not Mineself. I am the Giver and the Taker; the Sower and the Reaper. I have sent thee forth as ones of free will - now I shall bring thee back, as ye are prepared.

Say unto them which seek the Light, that it shall not be hidden - they have but to look and see, and be One with IT, for IT is the Everlasting and Eternal Light which never fails. All else shall pass away, but the Light shall remain Always.

Bargain not with IT, for it knows no less than Itself, Its own likeness - that which is of the Light shall not perish or pass away.

It is said, Mine Word shall not pass away; it is from ever-lasting to everlasting - Eternal Truth; knows no end, for there is no beginning - It has always been. I say, be ye as One with It, and know ye the true from the false, which shall pass as the chaff in the winds.

Come ye hither; stand with Me upon Mine solid Foundation, and the winds which blow foul, shall not touch thee, neither shall the smoke be found within thine garments, for they shall be white as the snow, and pure as the first-born of Him which hast sent thee forth.

Let not the debris of time, and the foulness of darkness touch thee, for it is come when ye shall stand before the Mighty Council as one accountable.

Accountable, I say! for none shall judge thee without the accounting. Let it be well with thee; for thine own sake I have spoken; for thine own sake I ask thee:

Hear Me, and give unto Me credit for being that which I AM - so be it and Selah.

Recorded by Sister Thedra

November 14, 1976

The Two Banners

Sori Sori -- Hast it not been said that ye shall now take up thy pen and write that which is given unto thee? So be it that ye shall give unto them this Word, and it shall profit them to receive it. They shall be blest to receive this portion - for this is it given.

There shall come one from out the Light which shall lead Mine people out of bondage - and indeed they are in bondage - for this shall One be sent unto them. They shall cry out for relief, and they shall be as ones scourged by the oppressors and magicians which weave the web of illusions that they be scourged.

Now I say unto Mine people, Hold ye steadfast; waver not, and be as ones true unto thy own self and fail not, for it is now come when ye shall take up thine own cross, and ye shall go into battle as the soldiers of Light carrying <u>Mine</u> <u>Banner</u> - the Cross and Crown - while the enemy shall carry the banner of the "skull & crossbones". So be it that Mine Banner shall not be stained with blood, for O The Light shall bear them up, which carry Mine Banner.

There shall be great conflict and much sorrow within thine land, and it shall be as nothing thou hast seen. For there are ones which sit in high places planning their nefarious schemes; and they shall fall before Mine Banner, for I have said, Nothing shall prevail against it. And they shall be as ones set apart, wherein there is no light, and great shall be the stress of them which set foot against Me and Mine people.

There shall be no place for the aggressors and evil spirits which but act within their own way. I say, Their way is not Mine way - and they shall fall before the Light which I AM - so be it and Selah.

Wait upon me, for I am the Lord thy God and I shall lead thee out of bondage, and ye shall know freedom as ye have not known.

Recorded by Sister Thedra
May 5, 1976.

Effulgence of Light

Sori Sori -- There will be a great effulgence of Light; it will be seen by the masses and be recognized that it is not of Earth. And yet it is to be just another sign along the way indicating that this is the age of the signs that have long been foretold.

The signs in themselves are merely the precursors of the great changes which are to take place on and within your planet. Make preparation your watchword, that you be not taken by surprise - so be it and Selah.

The Wonderful Plan

Sori Sori -- There shall be great thunderings, great mutterings and much action; yet it shall not foretell of peace, for peace shall not be part of their thunderings and mutterings. There shall be no foundation upon which it shall be established, for it is not within them. I have said, Let peace be established within them - for they shall be first to establish it within themself - then the peace which they speak of shall become a fact, and their pacts shall not be necessary. There is none so foolish as to think their pacts shall bring peace within a World wrought with darkness and selfishness. Let them heed Mine Word and be as ones prepared for lasting peace - so be it and Sela.

Recorded by Sister Thedra
May 7, 1976

Sori Sori -- Be it the way of man to fail to see the handwriting on the well and recognize its meaning. The changes are ever present and all about him - still he looks for signs and wonders as his. man-made structures collapse in the dust. O foolish man, Awaken to the meaning and purpose of these happenings, and begin your own preparation, Receive My lord with open hearts and apply it to your lives, for the time is short - so be it and Selah.

Recorded by
May 7, 1976

Note: Severe earthquakes hit Europe this date.

Signs and Signs

Sori Sori -- There are signs and signs galore, yet I say, They see not, they hear not; and I say unto them, The time is at hand when they shall find they have slept Over-time, so be it that I am come - I am come that they awaken, and for this have I spoken unto them that they might know that which is at hand.

I come declaring the way or the Lord - and they turn their face from Me. They grovel for a pittance, while I call out saying: Come follow ye Me. They give unto themself credit for being wise, while they are fools, hence they do not know. Yet they speak much of peace - therefore I say, Let it be established within you ma and they heed Me not. Be ye as one which has Mine hand upon thee, and ye shall be as one blest, Let peace be thy watch-word.

Recorded by Sister Thedra

May 9, 1976

Purification of The Planet

Sori Sori -- Mighty is He who has come to bring the Word from the Father and to awaken His sleeping brothers in Earth. For too long have they slept, and their awakening will come as a shock to the core of their being. Prepare for the great changes that even now are upon and within the places of Earth. Although it has been described through many sources, man cannot conceive of the completeness of the changes attendant to the purification of thy planet and that which surrounds her.

As with any new birth, pain and suffering will accompany her for a time, but then soon be forgotten in the joy of the new life which she will bring forth. So be it and Selah.

Recorded by

May 8, 1976

Earth Changes

Sori Sori -- How their land shall be laid waste, ana nothing that has been built by the hand of man shall be left standing. It is for them to learn and know that only that which is of Spirit will endure. They

27

have not heeded My call to prepare themselves, and they shall be caught unaware, sleeping in their beds, and they shall find their preparation for comforts and security has been misplaced. Yet I shall sent teachers among them during their time of trial, and they shall then know the wisdom of My words. So be it and Selah.

Recorded by

May 9, 1976

The Great Shock

Sori Sori -- There shall be a mighty shock which rocks the land wherein they are asleep. They shall be alerted, for I say: They have slept overtime and know not that they are sleeping. Awaken! I say unto them, Awaken! and they hear Me not. So be it they shall be as ones which have been alerted - yet they go to sleep on their feet; I cry unto them, yet they heed not. Now it is come when great stress shall come upon them, and much suffering shall be their lot - so be it and Selah. There shall be One sent amongst them that they find comfort; that they might not surfer more - and for this am I come, yet one shall go out before Me that they be prepared to receive Me.

While it is yet time, I call out in a loud Voice, "Give unto Me that which is Mine, and I shall give unto thee that which is thine, and ye shall know no suffering, no torment." I know wherein thy torment lie, and therein, thine Victory. Go ye not into the dragon's den to find thy victory, for I am the Wayshower and the Deliverer, which hast watched thee and kept thee for this day. I say, Watch! Watch! Watch with diligence, and fear not for I am come. While the ones of darkness know me not by any Name, they deny Mine Word and fear that which I offer unto them - while the dragon gives unto them the honeyed words, which shall be bitter unto their stomach.

I am not a traitor, I am the One Sent of Mine Father, I flatter them not, neither do I give unto them that which would confuse there. Let them look, and see, and know the true from the false. I say, I give unto them that which is sufficient - and it is for their sake that I come among them crying: "Know ye the Truth which shall make ye free - hear ye and be ye as ones prepared to go where I go, for I go unto Mine Father which hast Sent Me."

Pity are they which mock lie, for I am not to be mocked. I am not an impostor, therefore I say: "Lift up thine eyes and behold the Glory of God which hast given unto three Life", and prepare thyself that ye be as one to receive thine inheritance in full. Know ye the Truth.

Forget not that there are ones which are fraught with confusion and misgiving. They are wont to know; they are bound by opinions, and the many voices which know not - voices from out the darkness, which seek recognition of men, Pity are they which are caught within their web - they also cry and wail from out the pit; too, there are ones who hear their wailing and heed unto it, knowing not how to assist them, falling also into the pit.

Be ye aware, and fall not into the pit, for therein is much torment. I say unto thee, be ye watchful, thoughtful of Mine Words and heed the warning from out Mine own mouth, for I tell thee I am no part of their nefarious schemes; no part of their darkness, for I am sent as of old, with the Light which lightens every man's way, which accepts the Light which is his by divine right. I am come that he might know himself, that which is his divine inheritance. I offer him only freedom - salvation from bondage.

List unto Me, ye which loot in dark places for thy salvation. I say, ye find it not among the unknowing ones; the flatterers; the ones which offer the bitter cup, which they gild and sweeten that it be palatable unto thee; these the deceivers; the traitors which lay the traps for the unsuspecting ones. Pity are they who know not the deception! Gross are their ways; pity their plight - wast it not ever thus?

I say, behold ye the Light, and weary not, fret not - and ye shall know as I know, for I AM the Light of the world - Amen and Amen.

Recorded by Sister Thedra

May 18, 1976

Sori Sori -- I am come, I AM COME! Unto them which are prepared to receive Me, and unto them which are not prepared, I say "Prepare thine self and I shall reveal Mineself unto thee". So be it that I am sent that the way be prepared that ye might return unto the Father with Me - for this hast He sent Me.

Now I say unto all, that which is prudent and lawful; I betray not Mineself or Mine trust, for I am given unto the way of the Initiate. I fall not before their onslaught; I fail not, neither do I quail before their unfaithfulness, their hypocrisy. I ask of them naught other than they awaken, look, see, and understand. So be it that the unbelievers shall stand still, and they shall not be moved by Mine Calls or by that which I do - for they are bound within the dragon's den, and for the most part they are his pains, knowing not that he has bound them.

30

He whispers gentle words of flattery; promises of great glory; then he forsakes them on the brink of the pit, without hope and in despair.

"He" inspires them to mimic Me, to set foot against Mine servants, and they delight in so doing. So be it I see and knot that which they do, and for this I am prepared. I say, not ono which misuses Mine Hord, or Mine servants, shall abide with Me - neither shall they enter into Hine house. For this shall they prepare themself. And have I not said: "Come follow me, that ye might go where I go"? Therein is eternal freedom,

Know ye not that the magician is known unto Me? The one which hast bound the uninitiated, hast held thee within his spell, that ye might do his will/ his bidding, for from the beginning has he set foot against Me.

Now ye shall know the TRUE from the false, when ye so choose the Light which I AM.

Ye shall walk the way I shew unto thee, and ye shall fall not prey unto the fowler's snare.

Behold ye the Way and walk ye therein; lift up thine feet and ye shall not fall before his temptations, for I shall guide and direct thee, Ye shall carry thine own cross; be responsible lor thine own self and obey the law which I give unto thee this day - for this is the day long foretold. Why wait ye longer? Why wait?! I say, I am come unto them which are prepared to receive Me.

Hear ye that which I say. Take heed and I shall reveal unto the humble, true, and just, that which ye have not known. Put aside all thine preconceived ideas of Me and about Me, and let thine mind be staid on Truth and Justice, and I shall touch thee.

So be it I am the Lord thy God, known unto them in the realm of Light as Sananda.

Recorded by Sister Thedra

May 27, 1976

Why Thy Stupidity?

Sori Sori -- While it is yet time I say unto thee, give unto them this word, for it is now come when they shall be sorely oppressed, and they shall cry out for relief; they shall find that they have forfeited their inheritance, and the pity of it!

While I have spoken unto them from the firmament; from out the mouths of Mine chosen I have spoken - yet they have belittled Mine servants; spat upon Mine written Word; and flaunted themself before the children of Earth, calling themself "great" and "wise". Pity! pity! are they. Now I say they shall be brot to account for their stupidity - stupid are they!

Mine arm is not shortened, Mine mouth is not closed. Sorry shall be the ones which turn away from Mine servants who carry Mine Word unto them. They shall stand shorn of all their glory, their grandeur (self-esteem) and bigotry ere they enter into Mine house, for all are brot into Mine place as they are prepared - and I have given unto them the law. They have wearied of Mine sayings, and they mumble the phrases that they have given unto each succeeding generation, which they have sifted and scrambled unto their own

32

liking. Now they are want to make these sayings their own - yet they know not the meaning thereof.

O, how pitiful they are. They are wanderers on the brink of destruction, crying out for surcease from their burdens, and they know not the true from the false. I cry unto them, "Put thine hand in Mine and I shall lend thee safely", yet they go their own way and create their own fears - they make for themself their torment.

Why O man, art thou so stupid? When I say unto thee, thou art in the world of men as ones to learn the greater things, that ye be prepared to go where I go, Yet ye deny Me and Mine Word. Know ye that I am the one sent that ye be delivered out, that ye find thy way back unto thine home of eternal Light.

I am come, why wait longer, why fear? For I am thy Benefactor sent to bring thee home. Know ye that I am the Lord God, and I am not to be denied. Let these Mine Words penetrate the darkness, and see ye the hand of God move.

Be ye alert les ye fall into the pit - I say, "Lest thou fall into the pit." Be ye blest to receive Me, the One sent that ye be blest.

Recorded by Sister

June 10, 1976

Warning Before Destruction

Sori Sori -- There is a time and a place for all things, it is now time for ye to take up thy pen and write that which I say unto thee, for it is the time of action. There shall be great stirrings which shall awaken many which now sleepeth. These sleepers shall sleep on, knowing not that Mine hand moveth as a mighty and loving hand.

Where there is Love there is Mercy and Justice. There shall be Mercy and Justice in Mine actions and all that I do, yet the time is come to separate the true from the false, and nothing shall be hidden from Me.

There shall be a mighty on-rush of water, and a mighty wind shall hurl the waters to and fro, causing many to flee and cry out in their anguish and misery. While I say unto them NOW, be ye as ones prepared, they rush headlong in their folly, hearing not Mine Words - these shall be caused to remember this Mine Word. I have said so many times, "Turn from thine willful way and seek the Light which I AM."

They fear, and profane the name which I have revealed unto them; they care not for the WORD neither the name. They slander Mine servants and belittle them - yet they, Mine servants shall walk tall in Mine sight; and these shall be rewarded for their loyalty and service unto the Light. Be ye as one which has the mind to know them by their fruit - I have said, "Ye shall know them by their fruit," so be it.

NOW I have spoken again or the on-rush of waters, the winds which shall blow and the power of the wind; and ye have gone in thy own way, heeding not. Yet ye wanton ones shall run, and cry for mercy and relief. The waters shall roll over thee and consume thy dwelling places, and the winds shall lay low thy houses and thy places ye have delighted in. There shall be no time to run, no place to hide. Therefore I speak unto thee that ye might be prepared.

Harken ye unto Mine Word ore ye are overtaken in thine conceit and ignorance.

When it is come upon thee ye shall cry, Lord! Lord! and I shall hear thine pleas, yet ye shall remember thine own conceit and puny ways and ye shall know that ye have defiled the name of thine Benefactor, the Lord God, Sent, that ye might have thine freedom from bondage.

Ye shall be as one prepared, for I say unto thee I am come, I AM COME, and ye shall not fear, for fear is no part of Me, neither Mine children, for they know Mine Voice, and follow Me; and they are as ones peaceful, and they walk with a sure step. These shall not fail in the time of stress, neither shall they be cast out.

Be ye aware of these Mine Words, I come not to distress, or cause thee fear - yet I say unto thee, "I AM the WAY, come, follow ye Me and no harm shall come unto thee," Pray ye for Light, and understanding. Pray ye that thine eyes and ears be opened that ye might see, and it shall be done - Amen and Selah.

Recorded by Sister Thedra

June 19, 1976

So Sayeth The Lord God

Be ye as Mine hand made manifest unto them which know not, and say unto them that which I give unto thee to say, which shall serve them well - the ones who hear that which is said.

Ponder well these Mine Words, for I am the Lord thy God, and I come that ye be prepared for the days ahead. I have said again and again: There shall be trying times, and great shall be the stress of the peoples of the Earth. Yet they have heeded not that which I have given unto them that they might suffer no more.

I come that they might arise; throw off their shackles, and be forever free. Now I come as one of them; as one which has the greater foresight, and I declare unto them: There is but little time that they have to prepare themself.

There are none which knows the hour of the Coming; yet they cry from their pulpits; their way-stations; and they pray with a loud voice, with great fury and much speaking - yet they deny that I AM COME this day. Be ye aware that I am present among you. I have touched them which would have Me as a constant Companion; as Shepherd; The Wayshower. They have felt Mine touch and heeded Mine Voice; they deny Me not. While they have borne witness of Me, others have reviled against them.

I say unto all: The time draws nigh when ye shall remember Mine Words, and ye shall stand in wonderment; and great shall be the sorrow of them which turn from the Light.

I say, I AM SENT of The Father of ALL; from out the Center of Light I come, bearing the Cross of flesh, and crying as One who sees thy weakness and sorrow. I bring unto thee freedom; while ye refuse Mine Gifts, and deny Me. I say, ye shall ask; seek Me - Mine Light, and I shall touch thee, and ye shall then know that I am thine Servant of Light. So be it that I have said: Come - Come unto Me and I shall give unto thee that which I have kept for thee. So be it that no man shall pilfer Mine Gifts; none shall mimic Me, for I am not to be mimicked.

I am The Lord thy God; arise and come forth as one prepared to speak that which I give unto thee, and I shall put Mine Words into thine mouth, and they shall be sweet in thine mouth; they shall fall as the gentle dew upon the rose, and nourish and sustain them which receiveth.

Look - See that which I shall do! Prove Me, for I am the One Sent that there be established a New Order upon the Earth; that man might become of age – maturity; that he might be prepared to receive his inheritance in full. So be it that I have spoken, and this Mine servant hast heard, and recorded it as spoken, therefore she shall be blest - so let it be. I am He which awaits thine call. Put aside all thine willful ways; thine preconceived ideas of Me and about Me; accept Mine Love, Mine NEW Name, and Mine Word - then I shall shew unto thee greater things.

There is no magic about Me, neither Mine Works, for I AM the LAW. It is lawful that ye prove Me - yet thru, and. by, the law which I bring; which I have set down that ye might KNOW the law by which to prove Me.

O, man of Earth, thou hast looked into the pigeon-holes for Me; and thou hast looked in many strange and foreign places; but I say unto thee: I am not afar off; I am here, I am there, I am everywhere, for I am Omnipresent. Accept Mine Word - Mine hand I proffer thee; walk with Me and I shall tell thee wondrous things which ye have not dreamed of.

Praise ye the Name of The Father Solen Aum Solen, The Cause of thine being, and rejoice that this day is come.

Behold ye the Light!

I AM that I AM

Recorded by Sister Thedra

October 23, 1976

Hear The Wayshower!

Ye shall now take up thy pen and give unto them that which I give unto thee for them, for it is now come when the winds shall blow, and the waters shall cover the land which is now uncovered, and they shall flee for their lives. And the ones which flee not shall be caught up short; these shall be as ones unprepared, for they hear not that which hast been said unto them. I say, let them hear; it is said, they shall be warned before destruction comes upon them.

There shall be great suffering and lamenting, yet I say unto them: I come not to comfort them; I am come that they be eternally free - free from bondage forever - for this am I Sent of Mine Father. There shall be ones which do hear Mine Voice, and heed that which is said to them; these shall reach out a hand to assist the ones who suffer; yet they but assist Me as well, for I have so spoken that they be prepared to do that which I shall give unto them to do.

There shall be One Sent to give unto them the WORD, and it shall profit them to hear and heed the warning. It hast been said: Look - Listen - See - and be alert unto Mine Voice, Mine touch, for unto these which are alert unto the Word which I give unto them, I shall quicken them and they shall know whom they serve. So be it that I come not to comfort, for comfort shall be short lived - I come that they have Light, Life more abundantly; that they might return unto their rightful estate with Me. For I go unto Mine Father, even as I cone; and no man shall say unto Me, Stay - for there are none amongst thee that knowest from whence I come - I am come that ye might come to KNOW.

Prepare thine Self and I shall hear thine supplications and heed thine pleas.

Forget not that I am the Wayshower; I am the One which hast heard thine pleadings; seen thine travails and sufferings. Yet, hast thou learned that which thou hast come into flesh to learn that there is greater things than ye now know; that ye are not alone; that ye are not strangers unto Me?

I ask thee: Have ye sought the Light that never fails? Hast thou lived the life of the Initiate? Hast thou loved thine neighbor as thine own self?

Why art thou so sluggish, so gluttonish? Why art thou such poor spirited? Why art thou so backward?

Ye walk backward, looking backward. Ye fall into the ditch where ye find only darkness and despair - while I cry from the heights, "Come follow ye Me" - then ye turn thine face and stop thine ears, close thine eyes, and fear that ye are being misled!! How thinkest thou, ye poor foolish children of men!? What sort of reasoning is this? I say, I am Sent that ye find thine way back into the Father's House.

Yet, ye have gone headlong into the pit of darkness wherein ye are, and wherein ye shall find no other way out, save by <u>Mine Grace</u>. For this have I come; for this am I speaking out this day.

I speak in a loud Voice and I wait thine ear - and thine hand ye shall freely give unto Me, and I shall stand by thee and lead thee into the Eternal Light. The light of the New Day is now dawning, and ye have but to be aware of it, and accept Mine hand, and ye shall have no cause for suffering or fear.

Blessing upon them which come unto Me with a contrite heart and a willing hand. These are Mine servants which have come into flesh that there be Light amongst the unknowing ones. I have said many times, I bring with Me a Host, the ones which carry the lamp of freedom - these are the Angelic Host. I say, some speak of the "Host", knowing not which they say - I would that ye all know the "Host", for they are not of the Earth - never were they - they are of the Angelic Kingdom of Light-Realm.... And wherefrom cometh these spurious words which try to mimic Mine? From whence cometh these voices? From out the shadows they come! They are the deceivers from the realms of darkness, the false gods - I say, they are not of Mine Realm.

I have spoken out freely from Mine vantage point for the good of all mankind. So let it profit thee to hear and be enlightened, for I am Sent that it be so - so let it be Amen and Selah

Recorded by Sister Thedra

40

Armageddon

Sori Sori -- Say unto them, that there shall be a great uprising, and there shall be great fear and want, for the they have gone headlong into battle - the battle of Armageddon is NOW in full sway. They need not quibble with words, neither their learned phrases, for I say unto thee, the battle rages!!

And for this I call unto Mine, own to stand prepared for that which I shall give unto them to do. There is work a-plenty to be done, and none need sleep longer, for I cry unto them, "AWAKEN"! Yet I see them indulging themself in their own desires and willfulness.

I say: Give unto Me thine time and thine whole attention, and ye shall be rewarded in like measure - for this have I said: Come unto Me willingly; and freely ye come, and freely ye receive - so be it and Selah.

Hear ye, and rejoice that ye have heard.

Recorded by Sister Thedra

October 28, 1976

For Their Sake

Sori Sori -- Ye shall put thine hand to the pen this day, and I shall give unto thee that which I would have them know. It is for their sake that I call thee out from among them which are in darkness, doubt, and confusion.

Now I speak unto them which are doubting and confused - I say: Listen unto Me and know ye that I am come; I AM COME! Therefore I ask of thee: Why wait longer, why suffer the torment which ye give unto thyself? There is but this day, and I am here, as well as there - so why seek ye in far places?

There are those which know Me - these walk with Me; and some are sent from the realms of Light that the doubting and confusion might end; that ye be prepared to receive Me. I shall come unto each one, when and as they are prepared. I have said, Prepare thyself to receive Me, for I go not into the dragon's den. I go not into the dragons den! - ye shall seek Me out and I shall not hide Mineself from thee.

When ye have found thyself prepared and approved, ye shall be given a plan, and the plan is perfect; not one plan goes astray - the law gives unto thee the explicit way in which ye shall find Me - then I shall say unto thee: Come hither and walk with Me, sup with Me; partake of Mine "Bread", the Bread of Life - ye shall find thine hunger shall be satisfied, thy longing no more. Put forth thine effort that ye live the law; that ye watch thine step; thine tongue. Put not thine foot into the trap which is baited by the dragon. Watch that ye get not caught up in thine own trap - the frivolity and wanton.

The times spell out Mine coming. I have promised thee long ago that I shall come again, bearing Mine New Name. Dost thou accept it? Dost thou trust Me, The Son Sent of God The Father? Dost thou pretend to know Me? Dost thou know the truth of Mine Being? Hast thou lived the LAW which I bring unto thee? Why pretend that thou hast Mine approval for thine behavior, thine deportment? Hast thou crawled upon the ground as the serpent, and forgotten that I am nearer than thine hand, thine feet? Hast thou forgotten the Vow to serve the Light? Wherein is thine conceit? It is surely not of Me, for I have given unto thee of Mine own Self that ye might see thine own foulness, or, thine own light. I say: Come ye out from among them which surrender up themself to the forces of darkness.

Weary not of Mine Words, for they are powerful, and therein is strength and power - use it not for thine own downfall, for therein is blasphemy.

O ye of little comprehension, I call unto thee: Put thine hand to the plow and look not back, for I go before thee that ye lose not thy way home, wherein The Father abides.

I beckon thee hence - I AM The Lord thy God. So shall it ever be.

Recorded by Sister Thedra

October 30, 1976

Sori Sori -- There shall be a change in the world, for there is one which hast prepared himself for that which shall be done, and he shall do it well.

Yet he shall be besmirched and harassed by the population which are the trouble makers. And he shall not want, for I say unto them, They shall see the change, for it is said that "One shall be Sent", and it is so - so shall this one lead them out of darkness.

Time Now to Prepare

Sori Sori-- Ye shall now give unto them this WORD, for it shall be part of their preparation for the on-coming days. While it is yet time, I say unto them: "Prepare thyself, the way is now open unto thee, and for this have I come into the world of men".

I AM COME! I am Come, yet ye hear not Mine Call: "Come as one prepared to receive Me".

There is not time to dance, drink, and make merry. While I do say, drink ye from the fountain of eternal bliss - I say, rejoice that the time is now, that you might receive Me unto thyself - when ye are prepared to receive Me.

Art thou prepared? Where goest thou - what sayeth thou? Hast thou been discreet in all thy days - and way?

I say unto thee, be as one prepared, and I shall enter in and give unto thee sufficiently.

Bless thyself - I ask of thee naught save obedience unto the law which I give unto thee. Heed Mine Word and I shall give unto thee Greater blessings.

"Sori Sori" hast been given unto this, Mine hand made perfect, and for this have I called her out from among the throng. So there shall be no mistake, it is for her - none other - that I speak the Word "Sori Sori". Be not mistaken, for this is Mine to give - hers to take. Be ye discreet in things which I give unto thee, and force not the Spirit.

I am a willing Servant of Mine children, yet I give unto then that which should prepare them to receive Me.

Bless thine own self, that I might come in and sup with thee - so be it as ye will it.

Wait upon Me, The Lord God, and I shall remember thee in the hour of thine trials and temptations.

Recorded by Sister Thedra

November 5, 1976

The Power That Grinds, Also Lifts

-- I am come that there be Light - So shall IT go forth as a Mighty River. It shall clean away the debris and make new that which hast been as the stones which hast ground the few which have followed Me. I say: The few which hast followed Me, have been ground by the same power that hast lifted them up.

While there are those who have misused this power, I say, the same power shall lift them up - What Power! What Power? they ask. I say, the same power that hast ground them down, shall lift them up - there is but ONE POWER! Yet it is for the most part misused by the populace.

Now it is come when they shall use the power to lift themself - each unto himself - each in his own way. None shall be left without hope. While they find themself in a state of confusion, I stand ready to lead them out of darkness or bondage.

Put thy hand in Mine and follow where I lead thee. I have said: "Follow ye Me - prove Me" - I am thy Friend and Counselor; I am the Way and the Light.

Come, and I shall shew thee greater things than thou hast imaged.

Recorded by Sister Thedra

November 6, 1976

Heed Ye Well!!

Sori Sori -- Say unto "them" as I would say, that there are many distractions which are put within their way. While it is given unto them to be beguiled by the distractions which cause them to forget the words spoken in Wisdom and Love - it is at this point where the enemy enters in with great delight, and he puts his seal upon them when they least expect it.

Now these have thought themself above reproach, and thought to follow Me - it is for this that I say unto them: I go not into the dragon's den - I am not of them.

I say unto the ones which have thought to follow Me: Heed ye well that which I say unto thee this day. I am no part of their frivolity and foolishness. The time is very near when they shall cry out:

46

"Lord! Lord! where was I when Ye called and I heard Ye not"? I heard not the call, yet I have said, "Be ye alert and watchful, lest ye be caught unaware."

While ye are paying court unto the ones which hear not, ye are not of a mind to listen unto Mine Voice. It is said that there are many pitfalls - where are they? Ye have found them; ye have seen them; ye have had them pointed out, one at a time! Now I ask thee, Where have ye added one iota unto thy stature? Hast thou given unto Me credit for knowing that which I have said unto thee? Put not thine hand unto Mine mouth, for I am not to be silenced. I am The Wayshower; I have spoken for the good of all - yet them which heed Mine Words shall be Mine hand and Mine foot; they shall walk in the way I point; they shall walk becomingly in Mine sight.

They shall not be blown about by the foul winds, neither shall they drink at the table of the dark one, for he hast set it with many poisons; with great care hast he disguised his fare, that ye might find the "idiot's delight", Shall I find thee wanting? Shall I find thee in the field asleep?

Watch! Look! See! Be ye thoughtful of these Mine Words. Turn not lightly from Me, for I AM SENT that ye be found and brot out.

I say, do ye as ye will - yet ye have had much; yet, there is more, which ye have not known.

So be it I am the Wayshower, I AM HE - I AM that I AM. -

Selah

Recorded by Sister Thedra

47

November 14, 1976

Revelation last night: Tacks - millions of tiny, sharp ones - some larger ones which were easier to see, had been scattered on the "Workshop floor" - - I made a frantic effort to get them up - - T.

The Innocent

Beloved of Mine Being: Let it be recorded this day that which I shall say unto thee, and for this do I speak unto thee thusly that it might go into the records, that all which are of a mind to learn might thereby be enlightened by that which I say.

It is now come when I shall speak out on behalf of the Mighty Council, which sits in the council chambers for the purpose of bringing forth peace upon the Earth, and bringing about the deliverance of the "innocent". I say unto thee, the "innocent" are the ones which have no part of the slaughter and destruction; these which are innocent have given themself unto peace, sacrifice, truth and justice; I say they have volunteered to come in flesh that others might be delivered. These the "innocent" are Mine emissaries, Mine messengers, Mine servants, and Mine hands and Mine feet made manifest upon the Earth; for they do the work which I give unto them to do. They do that which they came to do, and they have been ridiculed, persecuted and martyred because of Mine work which they have chosen in the beginning.

Now I say unto thee, these innocent shall be delivered out before the great day of sorrow and suffering - ye shall say unto them as I would, that many stand by to give assistance. Let it be understood that there are none which shall suffer vainly, neither shall I sacrifice

48

one of Mine unto the dragon!! I say I shall not sacrifice one of Mine unto the dragon.

Behold the power of God, which works in mysterious ways unto the unknowing ones. I say they shall marvel and cry out, for they shall be caught up short. I say they shall wonder at the power which shall be manifest within the world of sight - the manifested world. Their thrones of power shall be overturned! Their seats of judgment shall be torn asunder and no longer shall they ride the backs of the oppressed and the innocent, I say they shall be brought to account for their wanton and rebellion. Let it be said that each one has a number, a color, a symbol; and by his color, number, symbol is he known - let it be said here, that color of skin is not that which is meant by color, for the skin is but the seen garment which is worn by that which is made manifest, and animated by Spirit. It is the Spirit which animates the physical vehicle which is the color; it scintillates as the diamond within the sun, each one bears his own color, his own light, which is his identity which he never loses, for each one which cometh into flesh is the manifestation of Spirit in dense form. At no time does he lose his identity in the realms of Light, even though he loses it in the dense form; this ye call insanity, let us call it un sanity, for they are not In sanity, not in harmony with their divinity. Let it be said that there shall be great stress, and many shall be as ones affected by it, yet I say unto them PEACE, PEACE, PEACE, let not the way of the dragon disturb thine PEACE; let not the hatred and the torment touch thee, for I have said, "I am with thee" - and if thou but know that it is so, ye shall not fear. Let it be for thine own sake that I say unto thee, "Fear not for I am with thee"; give not thine attention unto their going and coming and foolish

49

chatter, the yellings of hatred, and the fools which cry out against each other; I say, give not of thine energy into them.

Plant thine foot firmly upon the Rock which I <u>AM</u> and stand ye steadfast, and no harm shall come nigh unto thee. Rest in the knowing that I am with thee, for I shall not deceive thee, neither shall I forsake thee in the time of need.

I AM Sananda

Recorded by Sister Thedra

The Oppressor vs The Oppressed

To see is not to <u>know,</u> for thine eyes hast not been a true measure of things as they are in reality. That which is behind the manifestation is the reality; for thine eyes of mortal flesh but records that which things appear into mortal manifestation. Thine eyes cannot behold the glory behind the manifestation; thine finite mind does not comprehend that which is behind it, for it is infinite in scope and within the realm of Spirit, for all manifestation which is, is manifested through Spirit, even unto the magic.

While I say even unto the magic I tell thee, the dark ones use the energy which is allotted unto them to bring forth their illusion. It is given unto them to know certain laws which they misuse for their magic. While I say unto thee the law is real, the illusion not! While I say they shall be brought to account for their illusions which they have conjured; they shall come to accountability and make strait their own way; it is the law that they atone for all their misuse of the energy which is involved in their conjuring. They have bound them which have had a mind to learn and which had not the mind or strength of character to resist them. I say, these too shall be given strength to resist the forces of darkness which have bound them - they know not that they have been deluded!

Now it is come when I shall speak out against them, and I shall set Mine hand against the magicians which hold <u>them</u> within their spell.

Think ye well of Mine sayings and let it be known that I speak no idle words, for I am the Lord thy God come that Mine people no longer be oppressed by the oppressor.

Yet the oppressor shall remove himself and he shall be put into his own environment; no longer shall he have freedom to oppress the innocent which have a will to follow Me.

This is Mine Word this day - give it unto them that they might do with it as they will.

I AM the Lord thy God sent that they be free - so let it be.

I AM Sananda

Recorded by Sister Thedra

Yet They Follow Me Not

Beloved: I say unto thee there are ones which have many minds, many opinions and preconceived ideas, and these are the ones which have declared themself to be of Mine flock - yet they follow Me not. They have not found peace, neither have they found comfort; I say they have not so much as found comfort. There are many which declare themself free, yet they bind themself by their own thinking and by their own opinions. They have not given of themself unto Me; they cling unto the old with both hands, and wait for Me to do that which I ask of them; and at no time have I denied Mineself the peace which I offer into them.

I say, they fill the cup with bitter dregs and they shall drink it - I shall not deny them.

Yet I say, empty out the old wine and I shall give unto thee water more potent. Let it be said that they cry peace, peace, yet they have no peace within them. They live within the world of appearance, and they grieve for the flesh and pray unto an unknown God for mercy, while I say unto them: "Know ye not that thou art Sons of God", that I am come that ye might have thine freedom?

Yet they expect to find it through and by the flesh - that which is of the world of flesh. I say unto them, "Arise! Be ye about thy Father's business", and see that which I shall do, for I shall lead thee every step of the way.

Let not the way of flesh beset thee - was it not given unto Me to go before thee? I know the way, and it is strait and narrow, and the Law exacts of thee ounce for ounce, and it is not favorite of persons - it plays no favorites. While they say they follow me, I say their feet are slow to follow Me - they are as lead.

Such is my Word this day - so be it I have spoken.

I AM Sananda

Recorded by Sister Thedra

Symbols – Dreams

Who shall deny thee thine inheritance when it is willed unto thee of God the Father?

Wast it not given unto thee to be Sons of God from the beginning?

Wherein hast thou been? Wherein hast thou wandered?

Now in "This day" ye shall come to know these things, for it, shall be given unto thee to awaken from thine sleep. Thou hast slept and for this thou hast dreamed dreams which have not been real; these have been unto thee symbols of thine plight; symbols of thine flight into bondage; symbols of thine deliverance; yet thou hast not known the meaning thereof.

While I say unto thee the fantasy shall pass with thine awakening, and no longer shall such symbols be unto thee necessary; and ye shall awaken into the fullness of thine estate, and no more shall ye be tormented by the fantasies of the dream world - no more shall the magicians hold bound the Sons of God. I say the magicians shall no longer hold bound the Sons of God, for they shall go free - for this do I say fear not. Fear no evil for naught shall come nigh thee, for I am with thee and I have spoken the Word which shall cut loose all thine fetters, all thine legirons.

For I say unto thee thou hast "willed" it so - so shall it be, for Mine Father hast given unto me the power and the wisdom to do so.

53

So shall it be for the good of all - let it be.

I AM Sananda

Recorded by Sister Thedra

The Flesh - The Spirit

Mine Children: This day I say unto thee, there shall be given the Law unto them which ask for Light, and these shall not be denied; yet they shall be as ones responsible for that which they do with such holy Law, for it is sacred and woe unto any man which desecrates it - the Law being that which shall set them free; for by and thru the Law shall they be free.

No man shall duplicate the Law which was given in the beginning for there is no duplication and no way whereby he might escape the Law, for he comes under the Law. While he is within the realm of flesh he is bound by the Law of Earth, the Law of "flesh", and it is for this that I say unto thee: "Flesh shall no longer bind thee". It is but the earthly substance which is bound to the Earth by the Law of Earth - while the Spirit is not bound, it is bound by nothing. Spirit is not bound in flesh, never was, cannot be; therefore I say unto thee, the physical is but the vehicle used and animated by Spirit which is free, and at no time does Spirit violate the Law of flesh. While the flesh is subservient to the Spirit, Spirit is the doer, the seer, the knower; and the Spirit of man is awake at all times and it is fresh, alive, and sleepeth not.

Therein is thine salvation - I say, IT is from whence cometh thine strength, thine help, thine salvation. Let not thine unknowing trouble

54

thee, for I say ye shall come to know from whence cometh thine strength.

I speak into thee of the <u>Eternal</u> part of thee, that which has ever been and shall endure forever.

So be it I shall speak again and again - let it suffice thee that I know whereof I speak,

For I AM the Lord thy God

Sananda

Recorded by Sister Thedra

Each Season Shall Bring Forth Its Harvest

Sori Sori: While it is given unto Me to be the Lord thy God, it is given unto thee to be of the same order, the same generation the first born, even as I. I say unto thee thou art of the "First born" even as I, and no man shall deny thee thine inheritance. I have said unto thee, thou art divine in thine origin and it is so - so shall it ever be.

Yes I say thou hast slept; now is the time of thine awakening, and ye shall arise and come forth as ones purified and made new. Ye shall be as ones refreshed, made new, and no more shall ye sleep, for sleep shall hold no charm for thee. While I say sleep shall hold no charm for thee, too I say that there are ones which shall sleep on, and they shall not know that the <u>new</u> <u>day</u> is come, for they shall be as ones in deep sleep. And these shall be removed into yet another place wherein they shall sleep on for a season in which they shall awaken and come forth. Each season shall bring forth its harvest according unto the Law governing the season; so shall it be given each one to be put into his proper place and environment, wherein he shall abide for the time allotted unto his preparation for his next step.

Wherein it is said, "Each unto his own", "like unto like" and "As he is prepared so shall he receive".

So let it be, for I the Lord thy God has spoken unto thee of many things, and thine preparation is the greatest of them all. Let it be said that I am come that ye be prepared for the greater part, that is thine inheritance in full. So be it and Selah.

I AM Sananda

Recorded by Sister Thedra

On "Changes"

Behold the 'NEW DAWN" wherein all things shall be changed. I say all things shall change; change is good, let it be, rebel not against it! For change thou shall have thine new body. Thru change shall the Earth be purified and be that for which she was created.

Was it not said that, "Change there shall be"? So shall there be great and glorious change; and no man shall stop it for it is the Law of growth, the Law which governs progress; progression is the Law and therefore it is good.

See the hand of God move, and know that it is the power of the Word which has set into motion the change which shall come about within the manifest world. Let not thine heart be troubled by the

56

change which shall take place, for they shall be many, and at no time shall ye be left alone without comfort.

I say, take ye heed of Mine Words for they are not given unto thee idly, for I am not given unto idleness or frivolity. Give ye ear unto Mine sayings, hold high Mine banner and let thine own Light so shine that they might see it and be guided by it; let them drink from thine cup and be blest. So be it ye shall drink of Mine, for this do I give unto thee of Mine that ye might be blest - let it be.

I AM Sananda

Recorded by Sister Thedra

The Divine Plan

Beloved Ones: The time comes when each shall know that there is a PLAN, a plan which was designed in the beginning when thou wast sent forth as individuals endowed with life. I say all was according to a plan divine in origin, and there was a Law governing that plan. Yet man has lost sight of such a plan; he has not had the mind to know the fullness of it. While he has divided himself and forgotten his identity he has wandered aimlessly, knowing not that he was created in the image of God the Father. Let it be said that he which has wandered aimlessly are the ones which have had their memory blanked from them. These know not their Source, their origin, their place of abode; I say these have forgotten that there is a plan for their return.

57

It is now come when the ones which have a will to return unto their Source, shall be fortuned the strength and the assistance, for this have We come nigh unto thee.

While there are ones which deny Him, that He exists; and it is but the pity of their plight, for He is a just and merciful Father denying His children nothing - not even unto the lessons which they shall learn.

It is come when many walk with the unknown, unsung, uncrowned; for thy sake they come and give of themself that the plan be brought to fulfillment. I am one of them, yea I say unto thee I bring a Host with Me, and with great speed shall We bring peace out of seeming chaos. I say We shall establish a new Order upon the Earth, and we shall not forsake the ones which are of Our specie, of the same "specie". I say we are brothers and no man shall set Us against Our own, or We know what We are about; and that which We come to do shall be finished unto the glory of the Father which has sent Us. Take no mistake about it, the Sons of God shall not be sacrificed. While Ours is a sacrificial mission, it is for the LOVE of Our brothers that we come in peace, anointing them with oil, and giving unto them as they are prepared to receive. I say, they have long been under the black hood, and they are not accustomed unto the Light which We bring; therefore it is necessary to tread gently, that they be not disturbed beyond control or adjustment. These are factors which We take into consideration, and it is given unto Us to see the whole situation with which We deal. It is for the good of all that We come amongst them at this time, for there is great urgency at the present time. The time is propitious and many wait Our help, assistance, and they shall not be denied.

While there are ones of a malicious nature which would crucify and destroy Us; I say We are not so foolish as to be trap't by them, for We know their nature and their plans, which shall profit them naught. Their conquests shall profit them nothing, yet the way is now made clear that they learn of these things which have mystified them; and they have betrayed themself by their wanton and willfulness, their maliciousness, and I say unto them "Cowards!" They fear for their own being, they have no knowledge of their "Benefactors which have guarded and kept them from disaster in the past, when they have stood on the brink of destruction. Let it be said that We are the "Benefactors" which have protected them from themself, the poor foolish mortals!!

I am the Director of the present activity which is now becoming apparent unto the populace, and they shall awaken to find that they are powerless against the Love which We bear them. For they are as rebellious children which know not that which they do, neither have the mind to learn. Neither do they have the strength to resist the Light which We bring, for it shall penetrate the darkness, for this is the new dawn! Let it go forth into all the lands of the Earth that they might come to know themself to be children of God. Therein is our part, that they arise! Awaken into their inheritance - Let it be! For I have spoken that it be so - so shall it be.

I Am Sananda

Recorded by Sister Thedra - 2

John The Beloved

Beloved:- I speak unto thee this day, as one come unto thee for the purpose of giving thee this portion for them; and it shall be given unto them as it is received; and not one word shall be changed, for it is given for a purpose, which shall be revealed unto them in due time.

Ye shall be as my hand made manifest unto them, and they shall remember thee, and give unto thee credit for being my hand made manifest; for without thy hand I could not reach them. I speak unto them thru thee, and ye shall be my mouth and my voice, for I come that ye may be my voice unto them.

Wherein is it said that ye shall have a new part? So be it, and so shall it be. Ye shall be unto them all that the Father would have thee be, and blest shall ye be. Say unto them as I would say, that one shall go out from the Father as He - as the Father HIMSELF, and he shall be as ONE SENT of the Father, that there be Light within the Earth, sufficient to lift her up into the realms of light, wherein she shall be liberated from all darkness forever. I say: It is now come when all darkness shall be removed from the Earth, and she shall be cleansed forever, and she shall go into darkness no more.

There are now many within the Earth for this part; yet it is near time when one which is to come, shall walk the Earth as flesh made manifest; and I say unto thee: It is true that the one known unto thee as Jesus the Christ, is now upon the Earth made flesh, and he walketh as man, and he has within his hand the power to bring thee out of bondage - when ye give unto him the power and the authority, for ye have been given free will, and ye shall will it so - so be it as ye will it.

I speak unto thee simply, and in terms ye may comprehend; yet ye are of many minds - many opinions, and ye have the concept of man, NOT the MIND OF GOD. I say ye shall see with the EYE OF GOD; ye shall have the mind which is of Him; ye shall not be divided against thyself. Ye war within thyself, for ye are filled with many opinions of other minds, which is not of God the Father Mother. I ask of thee: Be ye not divided against HIM which has given unto thee being. I say be ye one with HIM; ask of HIM thy freedom, and seek knowledge of HIM, and HE shall give unto thee that which shall profit thee.

Be ye blest of me and by me, for these my words carry with them the power and authority of God the Father, and ye shall be as one prepared to receive the greater part. So be it and Selah. Praise ye the Father Mother God. Unto HIM all the Glory. I am sent of HIM that ye may come to know HIM in all HIS GLORY.

I am the Son called John the Beloved, so be it - and so shall it be ye too are loved.

Recorded by Sister Thedra of the Emerald Cross

Sarah Speaking

Beloved of my being:- Blest: art thou and blest shall ye be. I come unto thee that ye may have this my word, they which ye shall give unto them, that they may know that which I say unto thee. And as much as I say it into thee, I say it unto them, for are they not mine - have they not gone out from me as my breath made manifest?

And I say, they are now preparing themself for their new abodes; some shall remain with the Earth until the last hour, then they which are the remnant shall be lifted up, even as the lamb is lifted up. And I say: The ones which are not of the remnant, shall go on to their new places which are prepared for them, and they shall be in their own environment, and they shall be as ones prepared for their places - each unto his own, and they shall be as ones which have builded for himself his own dwelling place. For this I speak into them: that they may be about their preparation, for it is now come when they shall be alert and about their work, which shall be that of preparation such is their WORK. I say: They shall not waste the energy allotted unto them, in idleness and in waywardness, for therein is the folly of fools. I say it is given unto the foolish to have foolish ways.

I am not of a mind to reveal myself unto them, yet when they prepare themself, I shall speak unto them so softly and gently - yet firmly, that they be not misled, for I am a watchful Mother, and I speak as one with authority - and I am given unto wisdom and mercy. So be it I am alert unto thy weakness, and I shall be unto thee parent-protector, and the ever loving MOTHER GOD from which thou hast gone out.

So be it I shall await thy return with great patience and anticipation - such is my part. I am with thee unto the end.

I AM thy Mother Eternal, Sarah

Recorded by Sister Thedra of the Emerald Cross

Gabriel

"The One To Come"

Beloved of my being, Be ye as my hand made manifest unto them, and say unto them, that in the time which is near, one shall go out from the place wherein I am, and he shall walk among them as man, and he shall be as one with the Father Mother God. I say he shall not separate himself: from HIM, for he shall be as the Father made flesh. Such is the will of God the Father.

I say: He shall walk among thee, and he shall be as man, and be as God the Father made flesh. He shall be born of woman, and yet he shall not be of the seed of man, for he shall be born of the Father; and even as Sananda, Jesus Christ thy Lord, he shall be born of Earth mother, and of the Father impregnated, of Light Substance.

I say: He shall be as one born in the place now prepared for to receive him; and at the age of twelve years he shall go out from the cloistered place of his birth as man - of six foot, and a perfect stature. He shall walk as a Son of God, and he shall claim nothing of himself, he shall give unto the Father all credit and the glory; he shall do the Father's will in ALL things; he shall walk as one born on wings; he shall bring unto him all them which are prepared; and unto them he shall give a sign, and a plan - and for this has he been granted this by the Father.

He shall gather together the ones which shall make up the remnant and he shall give unto each a part, and they shall be instructed in that part; and there shall be no laggards - no drunkards, for each shall be as ones balanced in all things; and they shall be obedient in ALL THINGS - they shall be as ones blest.

And I say: Ye shall live to see the day of his birth. And yet few shall be as one WISE, for few there shall be which shall know of his birth - at the time of his coming; and of his going, all shall know, for it is then that every eye shall behold his glory, and every tongue shall sing his praise, every eye shall see him, and behold him in all his glory.

And I say unto thee, that he shall bring with him a host which shall attend him, and they shall be unto him his right hand, for there shall be a multitude which shall be attended, and none shall be turned away.

And the curious shall be confused and confounded, and they shall be as the foolish ones, for they shall not be satisfied. Such is my word for them at this time. I shall speak again, that they might be prepared. So be it and Selah.

I AM Gabriel

Recorded by Sister Thedra of the Emerald Cross

Soran

Beloved of my being:- Be ye as my hand made manifest unto them. Say unto them as I would, that there are many among them which stand ready to relieve them from their stress and strain; yet they are as yet not prepared to receive these Benefactors, which have come so lovingly, and of their own free will.

I say <u>they</u> shall be of a mind to receive them; and when this is come, they shall step forth as fellow beings, and as ones prepared for to give unto thee a hand, in love and with joy. They ask no other reward other than to be accepted for that which they are, and that ye be prepared for thy new part of the great and divine plan. Such is wisdom to prepare thyself, for it is nigh time when there shall be no more time.

I say: Time is swiftly running out, and ye shall find thyself outside - and wherein there is no comfort. And sad shall they be which are found wanting. So be it and Selah.

Blest are they which seek out them which are sent; it is not given unto thee to know them until ye have prepared thyself; then they shall reveal themself unto thee. I say they shall find thee - be ye assured of that, for they are alert, and there is no hiding place. It is by thy light that they find thee; they go not into the den of the porcupine - they go not into the dragons den.

I say ye shall be found, when ye have prepared thyself - blest shall ye be. So be it and Selah.

I come that ye may be prepared; so be about thy preparation. I shall wait thy call.

I AM thy older brother and thy Sibor, Soran

Recorded by Sister Thedra of the Emerald Cross

Sananda to Unit #3

Beloved ones, seeking to walk in the light of service and love to all life: - Thou art needed - greatly needed, and the time grows short.

Ye are not as yet prepared to take thy part; ye are being prepared to take thy part as fast as the life-stream will permit; ye cannot be processed beyond thy capacity to assimilate that which is given. The minds of all who serve must be pliant; all opinions must be freed from thy consciousness; ye must know, and KNOW that ye KNOW THE TRUTH only!

Be patient yet a little while; soon ye will know the glory ye had before the world was. Ye walked with thy Father Mother God, and knew no suffering - ye will again, and all thy suffering will be forgotten. Be ye mindful of thy inheritance, and ask of thy Sibors for all that ye need, to assist ye in gaining thy goal.

Lo I am with thee always; ye are never alone; thy silent watchers are mindful of thee - but ye must ask - it is the law.

I AM thy Sibor and Brother, Şananda

Recorded by Sorea Sorea

Unit #3

Sori Sori Beloved of my being:- Be ye blest of me this day, and ye shall be blest. So be it and Selah. I come this day that they may have this my word; and PRAISE ye the Father Mother God, from whom ALL came, and to which ye shall return.

Bless them which reach out; that ye may be spared the torment which shall be experienced by the traitors. I say they shall experience great and much torment, long shall they wander in darkness, for it is now come when the gates shall be closed. And I say: The call has gone out, and we have said over and over again:

"Be ye as ones prepared to enter therein"; and they stand with feet of lead, their hearts hardened, and their fingers in their ears. I say unto them - THEY SHALL HEAR! - yet it may be another age - when they have experienced much sorrow; yet it is better late than never. So we WAIT for the day when we might assist them, and blest shall they be when they do turn their face homeward.

I say unto them which do wait, that they shall be as the ones which betray themself, and they shall cry out in their suffering and in their misery for help, and it shall not come, for we thy Sibors do work unto the season; we are sent at this time of God the Father for this season - this harvest; and them which are not ready are as ones which refuse to awaken; for we are crying from every land upon the Earth. We stand waiting thy call; we are prepared for any call, any emergency, and we are not traitors unto ourself, neither do we betray the ones who give unto us their trust and credit for being that which we are.

I say: When they do ask of God the Father their freedom, and place within HIM their faith, He shall send one of HIS SONS unto them, yea, He shall send a legion of His hosts; and HE is ALMIGHTY - ALL WISE. None shall take from HIM HIS POWER.

He is glad this day is come, when the BRIDGE is formed. I say it is a two way BRIDGE, and we come and go, and we bring thee which are prepared, and we return thee when ye have learned well thy lessons. And let it be recorded herein, that many do come as thy Lord and Master Jesias / Sananda, known as the CHRIST JESUS, even as He - resurrected from thy so-called dead. I say: Many things are accomplished while ye walk about in thy sleep. Ye are in darkness and know not that which goes on about thee.

I say: Ye shall be alert and about thy preparation, and ye shall be as one illumined. I say: Great revelation shall be given unto thee; so be it I have spoken for this day; let it be for the good of all mankind. Blest are the hands which serve me.

I AM thy Brother and thy Sibor, Sori Sori

Recorded by Sister Thedra of the Emerald Cross

The Supreme Test

Blest of my being:- Blest art thou this day, and blest shall ye be, I am with thee that ye may be blest, forever blest. Be ye as my hand made manifest unto them, and say unto them in my name, that: Ye shall be as one on whose shoulders rests great responsibility, for therein is the supreme test of thy loyalty and of thy greatness! I say: When it is come that the days of trial shall overtake thee, shall ye endure, or shall ye faint and perish? I say: Be ye now prepared for the time which shall come. I say ye shall go out from the place of thy abode, and ye shall go into the place which is new and strange, and ye shall walk upright as human being.

And for them which are prepared, it shall be a place of great beauty and light, for each shall be in his own environment, which he has created for himself. I say ye shall begin this day to create it, and ye shall be alert, and give unto me credit for knowing that which I say unto thee, for I have the greater vision, and I am free to read the records.

68

I say ye shall be removed from the Earth into a new place, wherein are the ones like unto thyself in development, and ye do not escape thy environment. I say ye are thy own preparation, and responsible for thy own deliverance from bondage. Ye shall choose this day which ye shall serve - darkness or light. Be ye wise in thy decision. I am now prepared to assist thee - yet the preparation is thine! I point the way - ye walk in it; and ye shall blame NO OTHER for thy failure to obey the law, nor shall ye give another credit for saving thee, for there IS NO VICARIOUS ATONEMENTS within the realm of being - IT DOES NOT EXIST. Ye are the one to atone for all thy misused energy, and ye are the one which shall correct all thy errors, and err no more.

So be it that thy Sibors stand ready to assist thee in thy efforts; when ye have done thy best, we shall lend thee a hand in brotherly love, and with wisdom which is endowed unto us of God the Father.

I am with thee by day and by night; yet I stand with hands tied, until ye ask assistance of God the Father which has given unto thee being; and then by law, I am freed to give unto thee as ye are prepared to receive - NO MORE, NO LESS.

I am not a poor SON OF GOD - ALL HE HAS IS MINE to give, and when ye are prepared, I shall give unto thee as He has given unto me.

I AM THE WAYSHOWER, and I come to point the way. Walk ye in it and blest shall ye be.

I AM Sananda, Son of the ALMIGHTY, ADORABLE, ALLWISE FATHER MOTHER So be it and Selah.

Recorded by Sister Thedra of the Emerald Cross.

Never Again

Beloved of my being Be ye blest of me and by me, I am come that ye may be blest. And now I speak unto thee that they might have light. So be it that they which have eyes to see, and ears to hear, and a receptive heart, shall see and hear, and receive these my words unto themself, and they shall be blest. Know ye this: Inasmuch as ye receive my words, ye receive me; I say ye which do not receive my words shall not see me.

Never again shall ye put thy fingers into my wounded side - NEVER! It is finished - ye do not keep open my wounds - it is finished - it is finished. Ye which do demand proof shall go on in thy delirium, and thy own wonton ways; ye shall NOT go into the dens of the porcupine demanding proof of me. I say ye shall be confounded and confused; ye find me not in thy edifices of stone, which ye have set up, and named for thyself. Ye have taken it upon thyself to build them of stone and mortar, glass, marble, metal and all other available material. Ye have gone the long way to find me; yet ye close me out, and it is so!

I speak! And I know that which I say to be true; ye celebrate thy season of resurrection with a display of thy raiment; ye go into the places of worship - so called - for thy own gratification of pride! Ye are unto thyself traitor; ye are hypocrites, and I know that which ye are; ye are not an enigma unto me, for I see thy record - I watch thee.

Thy heart is troubled, and ye are filled with fear and misgivings; ye point a finger at my servants; ye betray thy own self. Wherein is it said: Ye are not of the light; ye are used to the dark, and therein ye are blind; ye see not the light, until thine eyes are accustomed unto it.

I have said unto thee: "When ye are so prepared, I shall give unto thee a portion, and it shall be unto thee all things, and ye shall be free of all bondage forever".

I have spoken, and I am a Son of God, born of God eternally free, and I say that which should profit thee - ye have but to accept it in the name of the Father Mother God. So be it my part to speak unto thee as HE would have me.

I AM thy older Brother, the Wayshower, Sananda

Recorded by Sister Thedra of the Emerald Cross

Beloved of my being: -Be ye as my hand made manifest unto them, and say unto them as I would say, that MIGHT IS THE LAW, AND GREAT IS THE POWER THEREOF. And SWIFT is the RETRIBUTION thereof. I say it is now come when there shall be GREAT and mighty repercussions from and by / thru the law, which has been set into motion by the MISUSE of the energy which is sent forth - in, thru, and by these Scripts.

Now it is given unto me to give these words unto thee, that they may come to know that the law is NO RESPECTER OF PERSÓNS, and it is SWIFT IN ITS ACTION. When the POWER is used to gratify the selfish ego of man; to prove their opinions and their plan; to be unto them their stay and their staff, on which to build up their theories and OPINIONS, WOE unto them.

Words are inadequate to describe the law; yet I say unto them which are taking away and adding to - that it shall be given unto me to see and to know that which they do, have done, and shall do. I say they shall be cut off, yea, cast out into utter darkness.

Now ye shall give these words unto them, and they shall go out before the date allotted unto them, for it is my part to speak unto them that they be warned, and spared much torment, for they are their own tormentors - and I say they shall save themself, from themselves. They shall be held accountable for that which they do; and when any indiscretion, any comment which is unlike LOVE - and like unto blasphemy, is directed into the GODHEAD, it is not within my POWER, by law, to prevent the results - which is swift indeed.

I say again: The retribution is swift indeed. So be it that ye shall be as one responsible for every word which proceeds out of thy mouth. Ye shall be as one prepared to receive that which returns unto thee, a thousand fold, from that which ye have sent out upon the eth. I say it picks up its kind, and returns unto thee ONE THOUSAND FOLD! and no man, woman, or creature can prevent it. Be ye what ye create for thyself.

I come that ye may have light - so be ye blest of and by me.

I AM thy Sibor and thy Brother, Sananda

Recorded by Sister Thedra of the Emerald Cross

Sananda

Beloved of my being:- I greet thee this hour with my hand upon thy head, and I stand as one alert unto thy part, and I say unto thee, ye are as my hand made manifest unto them in the world of men. I say ye shall give unto them this word, and it shall profit them to heed it, for it is my part, given unto me of the Father Mother God for thee - for them.

And I say: They are now in the days of OLD CYCLE, going into the new - yes, even into the NEW by many many days! Yes, years in thy way of calculating time. I say ye have come into the NEW - yet some sleep, as there was nothing else.

I say: It is the way of the dragon to give unto them portions to beguile them, that their sleep be not ended - yet they sleep a troubled sleep, and they are in lethargy - while we of the higher realm CRY: "AWAKEN! ALL YE CHILDREN OF THE LAND - AWAKEN".

So be it that our LOVE exceeds our PATIENCE, for thy time endeth - while our LOVE is everlasting. So be it and Selah.

I say ye shall AWAKEN! and ye know not the hour, nor the place, for ye shall go into deep sleep, and therein is the pity. So be it we give unto thee of our love - our energy - our wisdom that ye may be spared! So be it that ye shall accept us for that which we are, and ye shall ask for LIGHT; and yet ye shall follow the laws set down for thee.

I say again: We do not sibor fools, nor do we give unto babes the priceless jewels, who know not their worth.

I am now within the Earth as man; manifested as man; I walk with feet as man; I speak as man, and I am prepared to come unto thee as ye are prepared to receive me. Yet ye shall be as one free from all thy conceit, all thy hypocrisy, all thy preconceived ideas of me.

I am not the POOR BLOODY PRIEST! I AM THE SON OF GOD THE FATHER - the ONE SENT OF GOD THE FATHER that ye may be delivered up.

Praise HIS HOLY NAME, and give unto Him thanks in <u>all things</u>, for He is mindful of thee, and He has sent me forth that ye might find thy way home. So be it a glad day when ye return unto HIM.

I speak with thee that ye may turn thy face homeward. So be it and Selah.

I AM Sananda, Son of God

Recorded by Sister Thedra of the Emerald Cross

Solen Aum Solen

Blest art thou O My Child:- Be ye as my hand made manifest unto them this day, and say unto them in my name, that I AM the Father Mother Eternal, which has given unto them being, and they which I have sent forth of MY BEING. And ye shall be as My hands and My feet upon the Earth; as My voice, and My eyes, ye shall see Me in all thy day; ye shall see by night; ye shall counsel with Me.

Ye shall look within for thy being, and NOT afar. I say ye are ME, and I AM thee - there is NO SEPARATION, ONLY WITHIN THY THINKING! I say ye think, and it is so - ye will it, that ye return unto Me and it is done.

I speak unto thee that ye may come to know Me. And were it not so, ye could NOT BE. Ye speak forth that which I WILL, and ye receive it, and "THINK" it into thy image, and it becomes that which ye image.

Ye do not keep My commandment and "KEEP THE WORD HOLY". I say ye have adulterated MY WORD, for it goes out into manifestation perfect; ye receive it; and ye condition it into thy IMAGE - BECAUSE OF THY OWN THINKING. Ye are as yet not of MY MIND, for ye have closed thyself off from ME.

I say: Once in time which is no more, ye were one with Me; ye counseled with Me. Ye have forgotten thy inheritance; and ye have now been given a NEW DISPENSATION, whereby ye shall walk with Me this day. The gate has been opened, and the Bridge has been finished, and I say unto thee: There are many returning unto Me this day, and ye know it not, for ye are asleep!

I say unto the ones which are prepared: "YE SHALL THIS DAY ARISE AS ON WINGS OF LIGHT AND ASCEND UNTO ME, EVEN AS MY ROYAL SONS".

I say: There are ones among thee whom I have sent, that are now prepared to give unto thee the Waters of Life; and too I say: The Water of Life is a tangible Substance, made visible by My touch -

from and of Me. It is MY SPOKEN WORD MADE SUBSTANCE, and appears unto thee as Liquid Light - and therein lies thy salvation.

I say unto thee: In the WATER OF LIFE LIES THE SUBSTANCE OF CREATION – 'ALL THAT IS PERFECT'. So be it that ye shall drink this Substance, and it shall free thee from all dense form, all Earth gravity, all attraction of the Moon. Ye shall arise as one eternally free. Ye shall become a LIVING SUBSTANCE, AS LIGHT MADE FLESH, AS THE LIGHT OF THE WORLD.

Ye shall be as My heart beat, as My pulse; ye shall hear My voice; ye shall see Me face to face; and none other shall deny My words, for I speak unto thee as thy ETERNAL FATHER MOTHER GOD - CAUSE OF THY BEING. And because thou hast turned unto Me, I speak unto thee; and because thou hast asked for the good of all mankind, I have accepted thee. And I am glad this day that thou hast chosen to return unto me of thy own free will. For long thou hast gone from Me; so long have ye wandered in darkness, which has held thee from Me. My longing is great; My heart shall be filled when ALL MY CHILDREN return unto Me; and I shall receive them with gladness, and there shall be great rejoicing thruout my KINGDOM.

I AM thy hand; I AM thy voice; I AM thy breath; I AM thy mind. Glorify Me, and I shall receive thee unto Myself.

I AM THY FATHER MOTHER GOD, Solen Aum Solen

Recorded by Sister Thedra

76

The Eternal Mother Speaks of Love

Beloved of my being:- Blest be this day, blest art thou O My Child. Be ye as my hand made manifest unto them. Praise ye O my soul; Praise thee O my child; Praise unto the Father Mother God; Praise ye Him forevermore, Sing Praise unto Him; let thy heart rejoice and be glad. I am come that it may be so - so let it be. I am thy Mother Eternal.

I am Sarah, the mother of Abraham; I am thy Mother God; I am His part which is LOVE. I send thee forth in love, and with my hand I write that which is written. I speak what is spoken thru thy lips. I speak and it is prompted in love, therefore* I do not speak, for I AM LOVE.

I say that which is good for all mankind; I bless them by the spoken word. I give into them that which they can comprehend. I speak unto them while they sleep, and I cause them to hear me; yet they arise from their beds, and go their way, forgetting that which I have said - yet they shall be caused to remember it, and not one word shall be lost, for when it has gone out, it returns, bringing back its fruits, and with great abundance. Such is the law.

I speak unto thee of LOVE, WHICH I AM. I am the MOTHER, and I give unto thee my love, and I cause thy heart to overflow with love, and the joy of mothering them; yet ye shall not deprive them of their lessons; a lesson learned is a lesson earned - so let it be.

I give unto thee of myself, that ye may walk gently, and with dignity. Be ye glad for this day, and I shall touch thee, and I shall cause thy cup to spill over - so let it be. Sarah

Sananda

Beloved of My Being:- Upon this ground shall ye stand and declare for them their freedom. and ye shall be as one in authority, for I say it is so. SO BE IT, and none shall deny thee.

So be it that I am He which is sent to do the will of the Father, and it is by HIS WILL that I have ordained thee in the PRIESTHOOD OF MELCHEZEDEK - I say that ye are as one ordained of GOD THE FATHER; that ye have been given the authority and the power to go out among them, and to speak the words which HE shall put into thy mouth. And HE shall speak and it shall become.

I say unto thee: HE shall speak and it shall be done - so let it be. I say it is true - so let it be, and no man shall make void My Word. I speak with the power and authority given unto Me of HIM the Father Mother God. I bless thee My Sister of the Emerald Cross.

I now command thee to give them this document, and it shall go on record as my authority of GOD THE FATHER, and I give unto thee as He gives unto Me - such is My divine right. I say it is so - so be it, and be it so and Selah.

Ye shall henceforth from this day forth, wall in My footsteps, and ye shall be as My hand, and My foot upon the Earth, and I shall be with thee into the end.

I AM thy Sibor and thy older Brother, Sananda

Sign thyself thusly*

Recorded by Sister Thedra*

He is Come

Be ye this day twice blest, for I come unto thee as thy Brother from out the Temple of Light. I speak unto thee upon a subject dear unto my heart; I say unto thee: One has come into thy midst, unknown into the sleepers; and He walks gently - O SO GENTLY! yet He is all POWERFUL, ALLWISE, and is LOVE personified; and He has within His hand the power and the authority to create worlds, yea to people them. I say HE it is which walks among thee, and He has gone the long way to bring thee home.

I am not afar off, nor am I in darkness, nor bondage. I speak unto thee as a free man - free born of God the Father. I have drunken of the Water of Life, and I am eternally free, forever free. I speak with thee that they might have these my words, for thou hast prepared thyself for to receive Me, and for this I am glad, for not all are so prepared.

Now ye shall say unto them in My name, that one which has come into their midst walketh among them as one of them; and one which has the AUTHORITY and the POWER to give unto them the WATER OF LIFE; yet they shall be as one* prepared to receive it - and none shall deceive HIM. And be ye not a traitor unto thyself. Every thot - and ye shall watch thy words, thy motives - for I say unto thee: Ye are the reflection of that which is in thy heart. So be it and Selah. I speak unto thee as one which sees and knows thee. I am not a fool, nor am I from the NETHER WORLD. I speak as the Father would have Me speak, and I am not separated from Him.

Now within a short while the ONE which I speak of shall go out into thy midst as man. He shall seek out the ones which are prepared, and He shall find them one by one, and He shall give unto them that which shall prepare them for their work which is to be done in the time which is coming soon - coming sure as the dawn draweth nigh. He shall walk with surety of purpose and with LOVE. He shall be firm in all His dealings; He shall make no allowances for color, or parts**. He shall not frown upon the infirmed, and the unlearned. He shall give unto them as they are prepared to receive.

He shall be glad for HIS PART, and unto it He shall be true. Justice shall be within Him; He shall be as one upon whose head the Sun never sets; He shall walk with feet of LIGHT; He shall touch them, and they shall be changed in the twinkling of an eye.

I speak wisely for I know HIM; I walk with HIM; I am His Brother - His COMPANION - I am too a FREE BORN MAN OF GOD. I wait for the next visit - I then shall speak of another which is to come, yet this ONE shall go out before HIM. Be ye not deceived, and find thyself cut off, or found wanting - be ye not as the foolish virgins. I speak as a Brother, in LOVE and COMPASSION.

I AM thy Older Brother, Soran

Recorded by Sister Thedra

* Here Soran takes the individual from the mass, and puts upon him the responsibility of his OWN preparation.

** Positions, or stations in the world of men. T.

The Treadmill of Reincarnation

Beloved:- I speak unto thee this day that they may know me, and that which I say unto thee. They shall bear witness of these my words, and ye shall give them unto the ones which are so prepared to receive them, and blest shall they be. Ye shall say unto them as I would, that in the days just ahead many shall go into their new places of abode, as ones prepared for them, and there shall be not one out of his environment; yet I say unto them: it behooves them to improve their environment, for it is come when they shall awaken to find themself bound within yet another place - in an environment not unlike their present one, and they shall find themself bound still unto the treadmill of reincarnation - and therein is the pity! for a NEW DISPENSATION has been given unto thee, that ye might be free from this law; I say, that ye might be free from the law of incarnation - so let it be finished this day.

I come that ye might be free; and yet ye have not been unto me a disciple, and ye have not given unto me thy hand. I stand with mine outstretched, and with my open arms extended, and yet ye turn thy face from me, ye have but to open up thine arms - thy heart, and invite me in, and I shall come in and abide with thee - so let it profit thee, and ye shall be as a disciple; ye shall discipline thyself, and be mindful of me, and that which I say unto thee: and ye shall abide by the laws set down for thee, for they are sufficient unto thee; and I shall come in and sibor thee in the GREATER PART.

Now let it be said that "There are none so foolish as the one which thinks himself wise, and none so sad as the one which betrays

81

themself". I say again: "There are none so foolish as the fools, and none so sad as the traitors- they are the saddest of the lot". So be it and Selah. Pity are they, for they shall wait a long while ere they are given a NEW DISPENSATION, for the gate shall be closed, and they shall find themself outside, and they shall begin from the beginning. So be it and Selah.

I speak into thee that ye might alert thyself; and forget not that I am watchful of thee, and I do not say ye are hopeless; I say: YE ARE IN LETHARGY, AND ASLEEP, and I stand ready to come unto thee at thy call; yet ye shall respond unto me in this day, and it is most foolish to wait, for there is NO TOMORROW! and YESTERDAY IS NOT, and there is only THIS DAY which ye have; and that is not thine to hold, nor to give.

I say, ye shall arise and alert thyself, and be at Peace, and seek the LIGHT which is eternal - without end.

I am thy Brother and thy Sibor, Sananda

Recorded by Sister Thedra

Many Are Ascending

Beloved of my being: - Be ye as my hand made manifest unto them this day, and say unto them that which I shall give unto thee to say - and it shall profit them, for it is now come when there shall be great and many changes upon the Earth. I say, that there shall be many which go into their new places of abode, which are unprepared for the change and they shall be as ones confused; and they shall be as ones which have gone the long way - for they have not prepared themself for this way**.

And it is now come when many are being translated, and which are ascending unto their new places - free from all the earth's endearments; all the gravitation of the Earth; all the attraction of the Moon, and the elements thereof - they are free from all bondage.

I say unto the sleepers; they have been given a NEW dispensation - a NEW DAY a NEW LAW; and they shall stir themself and ARISE, and turn homeward. I say, they which do, shall be brot in; I am come that they might be - such is my part and such is the Will of the Father.

Has He not commanded thee: "GO FIND MY SHEEP?" have ye not gone out?! Have I not put within thy hands the food? When they accept it blest shall they be - yet when they reject it, PITY are they! I say I have called many, for many are given into my keeping, and I shall not rest until I have delivered them out of bondage; yet they shall come of their own free will - blest shall they be.

I say this day, that I stand helpless before them which close me out; I simply wait - yet they shall find the waiting hard to bear; they shall be tormented of their own longing, and their own way; and when there is no other way, they shall turn into the Source of their being - such is the law. I say they shall turn unto their Source in the last day. So be it and Selah.

I am with thee that ye may be prepared, and that ye may be my hand and my foot upon the Earth; for I am within the Earth as man, and many hands have I, and I shall remember them in the day of stress - such is my nature - my love for them.

I am thy older Brother and thy Sibor, Sananda

Recorded by Sister Thedra

*So called death - (The back door)

**The Royal Road – Ascension

Annalee Skarin calls it the Front Door

Sananda

Beloved of my being;- Be ye as my hand made manifest unto them this day, and say unto them as I would say, that this is MY DAY WHICH I HAVE CHOSEN FOR MY PART; wherein I have come unto thee for the purpose of giving unto thee that which the Father Mother God has WILLED UNTO THEE.

I say, the Father has sent me at this time that ye may be brot in. Ye have waited long for this day; ye have gone in and out of the bodies of flesh, as so many garments - shoddily made and discarded as such. Ye have slept for a time and stirred thyself, and rushed back into the world of manifested flesh, as so many unknowing ones; forgetting that which ye have learned in thy former garments of flesh. I say thy memory is blanked from thee; and it is now come when ye may have thy memory restored unto thee - which is the Father's will. So be it I shall be glad to do my part that this may be accomplished.

I am now prepared to give unto thee a part which shall be unto thee thy memory; I have the authority and the right to give unto thee a portion which shall be unto thee thy freedom from bondage - such is my word unto thee. So be it and Selah.

I ask of thee: "PONDER THESE MY WORDS, AND IT SHALL PROFIT THEE".

I am thy Sibor and thy Older Brother, Sananda

Recorded by Sister Thedra

Channeled thru Sister Sorea Sorea; -

Many walk in darkness, not knowing their blindness, and nothing will change them; they rush toward destruction, and naught can stay their headlong plunge. This ye see on every side; waste not thy time on those who will not be staid; rather give thy time to those who are of a mind to learn.

Thou are many hands made manifest unto these; they shall have their reward - twice blest are they. You too, are in darkness for yet a little time, but thy day will dawn in a blaze of light so bright ye will be dazzled; thou are led as the blind now; but soon ye shall walk with certainty and knowledge - this I promise thee.

I am thy Elder Brother, Sananda

Lift Up Thine Eyes

Sanat Kumara speaking unto thee:-

Beloved of my being: I come unto thee this day that ye may be given that which has been kept for thee - and it is for the good of all mankind that I come---

Now ye shall say unto them in my name - that they shall be as ones which have the law given unto them which is given unto US -- I say we which have gone before thee to prepare the way before thee have followed these laws - or the one law to the letter - we break it not - for we have the wisdom of the initiate -- I say - ye have been given the key to the Kingdom of God - if ye will but see it ---

I say: Will ye not walk in the path set before thee? - and ye shall be glad forevermore -- Rejoice that it is now come when these things shall be revealed unto thee - and ye shall be glad thruout all eternity that ye have been delivered out ---

Now it is come when great stress shall come upon all the peoples of the land - and they shall fall under the yoke of oppression - and I say unto thee my people: Lift up thine eyes unto the hills - lift up thy heart unto the everlasting Shrine - which is thy own light within the Inner Temple wherein ye shall go - wherein all things shall be revealed unto thee ---

I say this is the Royal Road upon which ye have come -- I say ye are now entering into the portals of learning - and ye know not what lies ahead of thee - and ye see not beyond the veil -- Ye go in and out from thy place of abode with no vision of that which is to come - ye are blinded by the veil of Maya -- Yet my people! Lift up thine eyes and open up thy heart - and - ye shall be touched and quickened - and ye shall comprehend the law - and ye shall walk

86

with surety - and with dignity - and ye shall not make a mockery of that which has been given unto thee for thy own welfare ---

I say ye shall not mock me - ye shall not make a mockery of the law set down befor thee - ye shall not give unto me the bitter cup -- Ye shall not persecute my prophets - ye shall bless them - and give unto them as they would give unto thee -- Ye shall give unto them food and drink - for they are sent unto thee even as I am sent - for as I receive of God the Father - so do I give unto them and they in turn give unto thee ---

I am now come that there might be great light among thee O my people - be ye alert and hear me! for I am come that ye may be delivered out before the great day of sorrow - I come that ye might be up and about thy preparation - that ye might be brot out of bondage ---

HEAR ME - HEAR ME! ALL YE PEOPLE OF THE EARTH! - I stand ready to give unto thee as ye are prepared to receive - and I say - ye have received little - yet my store is boundless - and ye comprehend not the fullness of the Father's House -- Arise and come home - O ye children of Earth - ere the great day of sorrow!

I am thy older Brother and thy Sibor - Sanat Kumara

Recorded by Sister Thedra

"Remember What Has Been Said"

Beloved of my being: Be ye blest of me and of my presence -- I come that ye may be blest - I give unto thee power and the authority to say unto them in my name that they shall be as ones brot of

87

bondage - and they shall walk in the way set before them -- With great joy and dignity shall they walk - and they shall faint not - nor shall they weary or well doing - for it is near time when great trials and temptations shall beset the peoples of the Earth -- Ye shall not be alone in thy trials and in thy longings - I say unto thee - thy longings shall be great indeed -- And shall ye not find they strength within thy being - which is thy eternal being - which is thy self unveiled ---

Be ye as one which can hold fast unto the Light of the Christ which never fails - and I say unto thee - ye shall find strength and peace which ye have not remembered -- Bear in mind that which has been said unto thee - and ye shall find the strength which will surpass all thy knowing -- Blest are they which hold fast in the time of trials and temptations---

I say ye shall be as ones alert and watchful - for too I say - ones do walk among thee which would torment thee - and take from thee thy peace of mind -- I say unto thee: Hold fast unto the law - walk ye in the way set before thee - and ye shall find strength therein and ye shall be given the comprehension of the Saints - which now walk among thee ---

I say that thy martyred Saints are now within physical form - they do walk among thee - veiled tho they be -- I say - the ones ye have called great - and near great - the ones which have suffered that ye may follow in the path which they have found - that ye might live in the temples they have founded - that ye might have the laws revealed - that ye may be brot out of bondage - I say unto thee - these are now within physical bodies - and they are prepared to reveal themself unto the just and the prudent -- I say ye shall prepare thyself for great revelation - and too I say - ye shall receive as ye are prepared -- So be it and Selah ---

I am with thee that ye may be enlightened of God the Father -- So be it my part to give unto thee as ye are prepared to receive ---

I am thy Sibor and the Brother - Sanat Kumara

Recorded by Sister Thedra

Sibor - Master - Disciple

Bor speaking:- Beloved of my being: I come at this time that I might bear witness of thy integrity -- I say unto thee: Thy hands are clean - thy heart is pure - I say unto thee ye have been true unto thyself - ye have kept thy own counsel - ye have gone the long way to bless them - ye have given unto them that which is for them - and kept for thyself that which is given unto thee -- I say ye have been faithful in all things - and ye shall be as one which has proven thyself trustworthy - and ye shall go out from the place wherein ye are as one prepared for the greater part ---

Now I shall speak unto them which are fortuned to read these my words: There are many called and few are chosen - and they which are chosen are chosen as ones which have qualified themself thru the ages past - they have labored long for their reward - and they have earned the right to call themself "Sibor" "Master" and "Disciple" - they qualified for each part -- I say that even the disciple prepared himself to become a disciple of the Masters - he has given himself - he has brot his hands - his heart - and surrendered up himself for that which the Master has given unto him ---

89

In like manner does the Master surrender up himself unto his Sibor and so on -- He has the will to learn of his instructors - he has the mind - and he does not speak spiteful - nor does he cast suspicion upon his so-called 'instructor' - he gives his love and his attention - he has been prepared for the part of <u>disciple</u> ---

And now I say with my Brothers - that as ye are prepared so shall ye receive - ye shall choose this day that which ye shall do -- And when it is come that one shall walk among thee as one prepared to give unto thee the 'Water of Life' - I pray that ye may be prepared to receive him and of him ---

I say - this is thy own preparation - and the law has been set before thee - ye have been fortuned this part - this knowledge - and ye have the gift of <u>free</u> <u>will</u> - and ye shall either accept or reject it -- But let it be recorded that when it is given unto thee freely and it is rejected - ye shall begin at the beginning -- I say - sad is the one which does betray himself - pity is he! Blest is he which does receive of the Water of Life - for he shall be forever free -- So be it and Selah ---

I am come that ye might be alert - and that ye might see and hear - that ye may <u>know</u> - and ye have to be thy own judge - which is the way ye shall choose - none shall trespass on thy free will -- I speak unto thee frankly and fearlessly - and I am responsible for that which I say - and none shall suffer for that which I say - and none shall suffer for that which I have said or done -- I am not of a mind to see my sibets suffer for my sake - yet I have said things for thy own sake which should alert thee -- I am the father of discipline - so be it that I am thy Brother sent of the Father and the Mother Eternal - I am Bor

The Gate is Guarded Well

Blest art thou this day - and blest shall ye be - for I come that this day shall bear fruit -- I give unto thee of myself that ye may be blest as I have been blest of the Father Mother God - and ye shall come to know me even as I know the Father Mother ---

My dear children: For thy chidings art thou stronger - and wiser shall ye become -- I say unto thee - I am not of a mind to sibor the wanton and the willful - yet I shall plant thy feet upon a hill - I shall place within thy hand a key - which ye shall turn at will - and ye shall be as one prepared to enter into the temple gate ---

I say unto thee: The gate is guarded well - and the gate stands threefold - and the temple is four square -- And ye shall find the center thereof and mark it well - for therein shall be thy abiding place -- Ye shall put out thy hand and I shall touch thee - and I shall quicken thee - and ye shall remember that which ye have done and said in the days of thy forgetting ---

I say ye shall remember all that which ye have forgotten - such is wisdom -- I say the temple is sealed - and now it shall be unsealed - and ye shall stand as ones unveiled - thy front-piece shall be removed - and ye shall be unbound - and ye shall stand forever free and ye shall be glad -- So be it and Salah ---

Praise the Father Mother which has sent thee out as themself - ye are ONE with them -- Only in thy unknowing have ye separated thyself from them - and ye have had thy memory blanked from thee

- yet I say - ye shall have it returned unto thee - such is the Will or the Father Mother God -- So be it and Selah ---

I am thy older Brother and thy Sibor - Sanat Kumara -- So be it and Selah ---

Recorded by Sister Thedra

The Call Goes Out: Sori Sori Sori

Blest be ye this day for I am with thee -- O My Children: Ye are blest as none other - thine is a part different from all others - in no age have they had that which is fortuned unto thee -- O My Children - lift up thy hearts - raise up thy heads - Hear Me! HEAR YE ME! I speak unto thee from the depth and from the heights - I cry unto thee -- O YE CHILDREN OF ALL THE LANDS OF THE EARTH - HEAR ME!

I come that ye may <u>not</u> go down into utter darkness -- O ye my beloved children - long have I waited this day. I say unto thee: This is the day for which I have waited - that ye might return unto me -- Be ye as ones which have ears to hear me - and a mind to learn - and give unto me thy hand - and no harm shall come near unto thee -- I say I shall bring thee out of bondage forever - and no darkness shall consume thee -- My children - I have said unto thee at this altar - that I shall bring thee out as ye are prepared - so be it - and I ask of thee naught save that ye may learn of me. It is necessary to give unto me thy heart - thy hand - and surrender up thyself for all thy opinions shall avail thee naught ---

I say - ye shall come unto me void of thy preconceived ideas - and void of opinions -- I say ye know me not! and ye can find me in the temple wherein ye shall come - I say - within the place wherein I am ye shall find me ready to receive - and I shall welcome thee home ---

I say unto them my children: Of all the lands of the Earth - I have not turned thee away -- Ye have forgotten me - long have ye gone from me - and ye have not had the mind to return unto me ---

I say unto thee - ye shall now give thot unto me - and ye shall ponder my words - and I shall reveal myself unto thee - and ye shall be glad! Great shall be thy revelations - and great shall be thy joy!

I am with thee and I am glad! So be it I shall watch thy progress and I shall speak unto thee many times - and ye which are of a mind - shall receive me in the name of the Most High Living God - So be it and Selah ---

I am thy Mother Eternal – Sarah

Recorded by Sister Thedra

*"Pearls without price" - "Priceless my gems"

The One to Come - Mother Sarah

Sarah speaking: -

Beloved child which is my hand made manifest unto them: Blest art thou and blest shall ye be -- Be ye as my voice unto them and say unto them in my name - and as I would have thee say - that one shall

93

come unto thee from out the great Cosmos - from out the heart of God the Father shall he come - and he shall take upon him a body of flesh - a body of flesh and bone - and he shall be as one come for the first time ---

I say he has not had the body of flesh and bone - he has not gone into darkness - nor shall he - for he shall be as one sent of the Father - and he shall not have his memory blanked from him - for he shall remember all that he IS - and all that he shall ever BE - he shall know - he shall walk among tree as one prepared for this day ---

He shall walk as one which has all power - and as one prepared to give unto them as the Father made incarnate upon the Earth -- I say great is this day - and great IS this day!

I say the heavens shall open up its doors - and they which are so prepared shall have free concourse into all the places thereof ---

I say ye shall prepare thyself for that which is yet to come -- I say ye shall be as ones prepared for that which shall come upon the Earth -- Too I say - ye shall see the fulfillment of all the prophecies which have been given for this time - for there shall be great and trying times when the water's shall flow upward - and the fire shall mingle with the water - and the thorn shall grow on the wheat - and the rose shall bloom from the oak ---

I say ye shall live to see prophecy fulfilled - and for this shall ye prepare thyself - Ye shall bless this day when ye have received me - and of me - for I shall send one out from the place of my abode - which shall gather them in which are so prepared - and they shall be gathered as the hen gathers her chicks ---

Be ye as one on whose shoulders rests the responsibility of that which shall be given unto thee to do -- I say each shall play his part - and for this shall he prepare himself -- And ye shall not fall - nor shall ye falter - for I say unto thee - I SHALL WALK WITH THEE AND I SHALL SUSTAIN THEE ---

PEARLS are my children - and JEWELS are my thots - and few are prepared to receive my JEWELS - and not one of my PEARLS shall go unaccounted for - for they are numbered - one by one - I know each by name - and I see them wherever they be - and I have suckled them at my breast - and I hold them close that they may not go in deep sleep -- I nourish them and I give unto them as they are prepared to receive -- I say I do not waste time or energy in vain - I am the Mother eternal and I know them which sleepeth - and them which are awake - and I too know them which are beginning to stir from their slumbers ---

Now it is come when many shall awaken - and they shall be glad it is over - for it is given unto me to know that which has bound them in the hours of their unknowing - in the time of their sleep -- Now they shall call out and they shall be heard and answered - and they shall be blest indeed - and they shall be brot in and refreshed and purified - such is the will of the Father ---

I ask of thee nothing more than accept my love and my hand - and I shall bring thee into the place wherein I am - and I shall rejoice with thee that it is finished ---

Praise the name of Solen forever and forever - for He has given unto thee being - and He has given of Himself that ye might be - and

He has willed that ye return unto Him this day --- So be it - and I am thy Mother Eternal – Sarah

Recorded by Sister Thedra

The Emerald Cross

The Cross - it is a Company - an Order of beings who work within the Brotherhood of Man and the Fatherhood of God - for the good of all mankind ---

And at the head of this group one known as Mother Sarah - the personification of Love - embodiment of all Mothers - that is: The Love of God the Father made manifest in mothers -- The blessed Mother Sarah is the Head of this Order of The Emerald Cross ---

And when one earns the Divine right and privilege to associate themself with this Order - it is the joy of all the Orders and Brothers of Light -- I speak for the Order - for I am one known as Merseda - --

Spoken to Sister Thedra of The Emerald Cross

Emanations of Deity

Born speaking:-

I speak unto thee from out the emanations of Deity - I speak unto thee from the fullness of eternity - I call unto thee from the depth - from the heights -- I speak of Spirit - I speak of flesh - I speak of that which eternally is - and that which changeth not -- I speak unto thee of that which shall - and does change - I speak of <u>change</u> and change is good - and shall be good ---

And no man shall stay the hand of Deity -- I say - no man shall change the LAW - for it is the law that all things within the realm of matter be changed - there is no staleness within the realm of spirit - spirit is the newness of all things made pure -- I say: All things which are within the realm of matter shall be changed - cleansed and made pure - such is the law ---

I say - such is the law of the Great and Grand Spirit - Father Mother God - which has called forth all manifestation which is made manifest -- I say - all that is now made manifest shall be returned unto Spirit and made fresh - made pure*---

I say it is the law which is given unto all the lands - all the countries - all planets - all galaxies - all peoples within and on all planets - all galaxies thruout the systems of all creation - all that which is created and that which shall be created ---

Now ye shall speak unto them in my name and as I would - that I come unto them from out the heart of God the Father - I come as His emanation that He has willed - that He has sent out as His pulsation - as His breath -- And I would speak unto thee as a Brother which as yet has not taken upon Self the body of flesh and bone –

I have not spoken as man - I have not spoken as one of Earth - I have not been born of woman - yet I AM -- I am unborn of Earth - yet I shall take embodiment thru woman upon Earth - as Earth shall I be born -- I say unto thee - I shall be born of woman - in the same manner as was thy Lord - known unto thee as Jesus the Christ - known unto us as Sananda Son of God ---

I say - in like manner shall I be born -- I say - one has been prepared as was the Mother Mary of Jesus thy Lord - the Master Sananda ---

I say - one has been prepared even as she - that she may receive me -- As a child of twelve I shall make my entrance into the world of man - and therein shall I walk and talk -- I shall bring with me a legion of the realms of light - I shall have a place prepared for to receive me - and I shall have a place within the land wherein ye are at this time -- I say the place is there - and it is now being prepared - and it is guarded well -- And I say - there are great preparations being made to receive me - and the hosts which I shall bring with me -- And when I shall go out I shall be as no man has been - I shall be different from all others ---

I shall carry with me a blue star and all which look upon it shall know me - and they shall be gathered into the place wherein I am - wherein I shall be at that place - wherein I shall abide - and they shall become part of the host which I shall have with me ---

I say ye shall prepare thyself - for ye know not that which is to be - that which shall come upon the Earth -- I say - great revelation is in store for thee - and great shall be the day ahead -- Blest shall ye be - and blest art thou -- Blest shall they be which endureth to the end—

I am BORN

Recorded by Sister Thedra

The Time of Stress

Sanat Kumara speaking: -

Be ye blest of me and by me - for I come that ye may be blest -- Ye have given unto me great joy - for ye have overcome that which has been unto thee a great and heavy cross - ye have been true unto thyself - and ye have held thy peace - and ye have given unto thyself credit for knowing which way to go -- Ye have gone the way set before thee - ye have given of thyself that they may be blest - ye have faltered not - nor have ye stumbled -- I say ye have done well - I say ye shall be blest -- So be it and Selah ---

Now let it be recorded that there shall be a mighty wind - and it shall be unto thy place of abode -- Many there shall be which shall look for a place to lay their head - and they shall be given the place - and they shall be as ones which have with them the children which shall be comforted in the time of stress -- So be it and Selah -- I say ye shall comfort them in the time of stress - such is my word unto thee - for I have spoken and ye have heard me -- So be it and Selah ---

I am thy older Brother - Sanat Kumara

Recorded by Sister Thedra

Love in Action

Beloved: I speak unto thee as one which has my hand upon thee - and I say ye shall be blest of me and by me - and I say ye shall speak unto this one as I would - and ye shall speak as I would in Love - for I AM LOVE I move in the Spirit of Love - I say: I AM LOVE IN

ACTION - I say I am come that all men may come to know me - and as they receive me - so shall they receive the Father ---

I say I AM COME - I walk in thy midst - and I speak unto them which have prepared themself for to receive me ---

I go not into the places of the dragon for entertainment - I play a lone hand! I am not deceived by appearances! I am not deceived by words - for I know what prompts them! I am not deceived by anything - for I am not a fool - neither do I sibor fools -- I speak fearlessly and wisely - I speak out of compassion for the foolish - for they are as the little ones - they know <u>not</u> how short the time left for their preparation -- I say Life is Life! no beginning - no end - ye shall remember this: "NO END" death is an illusion - no escape from the law! As ye set it into motion it shall fill its cycle and return - all thy joy - all thy torment! Pity are they which set into motion that which shall torment them - I say they betray themself - they shall be as ones which have thrown overboard their own life-belt! So be it I have spoken and I am not finished! I am thy Master - thy Sibor thy Brother which has gone before thee to prepare the way - so be ye wise to walk in it -- I am the Nazarine Sananda - Jesus Christ

Recorded by Sister Thedra

Each Unto His Own Part The Hundred and Forty Four

Sarah speaking: -

Beloved of my being: Blest art thou and blest shall ye be -- Ye have gone out from me as one which has gone into the Earth for a part which is thine -- All which are within the Earth at this time have

100

certain parts - each unto his own and no two are equal - alike - for it is as thy fingerprints - no two alike -- And for the first time I speak unto thee on this subject - and it is for thee to give unto them which are of a mind to learn---

I say - give this unto them which are of a mind to learn-- There are many within the Earth at this time which have parts in the great and divine plan - and no two are alike for they are "parts" - no one has the whole part - and each unto his own -- I say each has been given a part - and many have not as yet awakened unto his part -- And too - let it go on record that each is prepared for his part from the beginning of his going out - yet some sleep and are as the traitor - he betrays himself - he thinks himself <u>wise</u> and he turns from his appointed course - for this does he pay the price - I say he pays a pretty price - he ransoms himself from his own prison - he ransoms himself from the self-created hell - he ransoms himself from his own bondage---

Poor in spirit is he which turns aside from his appointed course -- Now when they which go out as ones called from the Hiarchi they are given "parts - and entrusted with certain parts - and as they prepare themself there are greater parts entrusted them -- And when they have been found worthy they are brot into the place wherein there are treasures untold - wherein they sit in council as "one"- and wherein there is a hundred and forty four of the learned - which are of the Royal Assembly -- And these which make up this Council are as the ones which have thy records -- And nothing is overlooked - nothing hidden - and no one is judge or another - the record is the judge -- I say - they which are called shall answer and they shall stand before this tribunal as the initiate which has prepared himself for this part ---

Now it is come when one from among thee shall walk among thee - and he shall find them which are prepared to be brot in before the Royal Assembly - and they which are brot in shall be as ones which have prepared themself in advance ---

I say the path is narrow and strait - I say ye have the key unto the gate - be ye as ones prepared for the greater part-- Praise ye the Lord of Hosts - for mighty is His name -- Praise ye His name all ye people of the Earth ---

I am thy Eternal Mother – Sarah

Recorded by Sister Thedra of the Emerald Cross

The Condition Known as Sleep

Sanat Kumara speaking unto thee of a condition known unto us as sleep -- When one is in lethargy he sleeps for a time - and awakens within the body of flesh refreshed from his labors -- And when he has refreshed himself he has a clear mind and a poised body -- And when he has a poised body and a clear mind he is receptive to the greater learning - to revelation - and he is as one of a mind to learn - he has the will to learn ---

When he is asleep he neither has the mind or the will - hence we refer to them as the "sleepers" - they belong to the sleepers' realm - I say they are asleep! and they have not the mind to learn - nor the will ---

102

Such is the mind of many which are as ones which go and come in the world of man - I say they are of the sleepers' realm and they care not to awaken -- And too I say - should the Lord and Master Jesus Christ - Sananda Son of God walk among them this day and speak unto them as he does speak unto thee - and unto all his servants which do serve him on their behalf - they would crucify him this day - they would spit upon him - and they would think upon new ways to torture him -- I say the mind of the beast is in them - I say they are not as ones prepared to receive him - and surely not prepared for the inmost place of the Most High Living God ---

Ye shall say unto them in my name - and with the authority which is mine: I am now prepared to come out from the place wherein I am - as one fully qualified to give unto them as they are prepared to receive - I say as they are prepared so shall they receive ---

I am not so foolish as to waste my energy on the foolish - for I have spoken for lo those many days that it is now time to be at thy posts of duty - up and about thy Father's business - and I find them as ones forcing upon others their own will - their own parts - their own puny words which they have pilfered from yet others ---

I say they know not that the "Day of the Lord" has come -- I say they are to be found prattling, as babes - they are to be found in the places of gaming - wherein they indulge their senses of pleasure - they seek pleasure - not wisdom -- I say they seek phenomena - not truth - they are blind as the male mole -- They cry for the things of Earth - they wander to and fro - bound as by their legirons - they cry - Lord! Lord! and they seek him not -- Such is the pity of man this day ---

I say unto thee - weep not for them - turn not - neither to the right nor to the left - but walk ye in the way which ye shall go -- Be ye blest this day and the labor of thy hands shall be blest -- Mighty is the name of Solen Aum Solen - praise Him all ye children of Earth - lift up thy eyes - open up thy hearts and receive of Him thy eternal freedom - blest shall ye

be ---

I am thy older Brother - Sanat Kumara

Recorded by Sister Thedra of the Emerald Cross

Sananda: - Hear Me! Hear me!

Beloved of my being: It is now come when changes shall come about upon the Earth - and thruout thy country shall be much sorrow and unrest -- I say that these changes shall bring unrest and much suffering -- And too I say - that there are none so sad as the ones which betray themself -- And in a short while ye shall see great strands of water wherein are no waters - ye shall see the waters dry up wherein they have been -- Ye shall see great pestilences rise up to torment thee - Ye shall give these words to them as I say them - for they shall hear that which I say - and they shall not spit upon them -- For they shall live to see the day not far off - When one shall place himself upon the throne which he sets up - and he shall call himself God - he shall decree that they bow unto him and pay him homage - and he shall demand of them human sacrifice - and they shall do his bidding -- Now I say ye shall hear me out for I am not of a mind to sacrifice up my own - I am of a mind to alert thee - yet should ye turn a deaf ear - I am helpless -- I cry unto thee O my

104

children - be ye alert and hear me! I say ye shall have trying times - and ye shall be as ones true unto thyself and ye shall cling unto the Light -- Ye shall ask of the Father - Light and Truth - ask for comprehension - and walk ye in the way set before thee ---

I say that the way of the dragon is a subtle thing - he would deceive thee and cause thee to be befuddled - he would give unto thee the bitter cup - he would divide my sheep and scatter them -- My children! My children! which I call my sheep - I say he would scatter thee - and confuse thee -- I say unto thee - be ye as one which has my hand upon thee and ye shall be led out of bondage - out of darkness - such is my word unto thee -- Hold fast unto the law set before thee and glad shall ye be ---

I am thy Sibor and thy Brother - Sananda - Son of God -- So be it and Selah

"Grieve not for those who fall on the field of service - for theirs is a crown of Glory....

"Know ye not that there are martyred Saints that walk among you <u>uncrowned</u>?

"I am come that ye may have the comprehension to recognize them -- Were it not for them I would bring thee into the place wherein I am thru levitation - it will be done - thru a closed circle -- "

Recorded by Sister Thedra of the Emerald Cross

The Dragon is Bound in His Own Den!

Sananda speaking: -

Beloved of my being: My hand is and has been upon thee -- I say I am with thee and I shall not forsake thee - I say I am not of a mind to forsake thee - and I am given unto watchfulness - I see that which goes on about thee ---

I say unto thee - the lash of the dragon's tail is but the ill wind which bloweth the stench from out his nostrils - he has been bound and he has his hands tied and he has no power to touch thee - And he is now incarcerated within his own den - and he is furious he has no power over thee - for from this day forward shall he be bound - he shall not come near unto thee -- This is my word - my promise unto thee my child -- Dry thy tears and give unto me credit for that which I am - and I say unto thee I am the keeper at the gate - I am thy gate keeper - and I see that no unclean thing enter into this port - I come into this port and I shall keep it clean - that I might use it for the good of all mankind -- So shall it be -- Be ye as one prepared for the greater part and ye shall be glad - so be it a time of rejoicing -- Amen -- So be it and Selah.---

Say unto them that they shall stand as "One" with one mind - one purpose - and they shall be as one which has the mind to serve the will of the Father -- And they shall be as ones ready for that which shall be given unto them to do - they shall be as ones prepared at all times to be called at the midnite hour - for in the time which is near there shall be a great voice ring out thru the Cosmos - and it shall be recognized by all which has alerted themself and prepared themself for this day ---

I say - they which are asleep shall be as the sleepers - they shall be found dreaming - and their dreams shall torment them - and they shall be as ones confused - and they shall be as ones frightened and without solace ---

I say - they which are of a mind to learn and which are of a mind to follow me shall be alert - and they shall be without confusion - and they shall be as ones which have my hand upon them and I shall lead them with surety and they shall not fall - nor shall they stumble -- I say they shall not stumble and fall - for I am of the Father sent - and I am not of a mind to leave my sheep unto the wolves ---

Blest are they which hold fast unto the law and blest shall they be - I am come that my sheep be not scattered -- Yet they hear the voices of strange masters which they would follow in the time of their confusion - I say they are as ones frightened and confused - for the day of sifting is at hand - and they call out in their delirium and they are as ones bound by that which they know not -- They have not the power within their own hand to fight off the beast - they have not the wisdom which is of the Christed ones - that which is of the Father -- Without their knowing they have naught - I say they have naught - So be it and Selah - - -

To know is wisdom - to think is uncertainty - and to think is not to know - I say therein lies the difference between belief and wisdom -- Man's opinions is not the mind of the

Father - and it is the tower of Babel which shall fall - it shall crumble at their feet - for they which think themself wise shall be found wanting - I say they shall be brot face to face with their foolishness -- So be it and Selah ---

107

I am responsible for that which I say - and no man shall call me a fool -- So be it and Selah ---

I am Sananda - Son of God

The One to Come Shall Take Upon Himself The Cross of Flesh

Sanat Kumara speaking: -

Beloved of my being: Be ye as my mouth and as my hand made manifest unto the ones which gather themself together - and say unto them in my name that it is now come when great shall be the activities within the Earth and about it ---

I say we which do sit in council are alert - we have our eyes open and we see and know that which does go on -- And I say with wisdom and with surety - that it is the part of thy guardians to protect thee in the hours of stress -- I say that there are no traitors among us - we speak unto truth and wisdom and we speak fearlessly - for it is given unto us to know the law - and I say we abide by it -- So be it that we walk in the way which we point out unto thee - and I say that we have gone before thee to prepare the way before thee - and ye shall prepare thyself diligently for that which shall be entrusted unto thee to do ---

Now let this go on record - that each has his own free will and none shall trespass upon it -- And when one comes into thee and inquires of thee - ye shall give unto him the law - and he shall choose that which he shall do with it - he shall be as one free to choose -- He shall be as one wise to choose to abide by it - he shall be as a

108

traitor unto himself to refuse it -- So be it the law - as they ask so shall they receive -- So be it and Selah ---

I say one shall come from out the east and he shall be as no other - and he shall be as one which has taken embodiment thru woman - yet he shall be of light - he shall not be the seed of man - and he shall go out from his place of physical birth at the age of twelve - and he shall walk among thee as God the Father made manifest in flesh -- He has not been born of woman (before) - he has not walked the Earth as man - and he has not taken upon himself the cross of flesh -- I say he has not taken upon himself the chemical form of animal man - he has not come into thy realm (before) - he shall - and ye shall be as ones to see him -- I say he shall bring great light - and all which are so prepared shall walk with him and see him face to face - such shall be thy reward -- So be it and Selah ---

I am thy Brother and thy Sibor - Sanat Kumara

Recorded by Sister Thedra of the Emerald Cross

As The Moth Which Goes Into The Flame

Sananda speaking: -

Beloved of my being: Ye have said that which I have given unto thee to say - and I speak unto thee as one prepared to give unto thee the "new" part - and it shall be new - separate - and unlike any other ---

Ye shall be as one prepared for this part - and I say unto thee - the "old" shall serve thee well - and ye shall bless the day which has been unto thee thy stepping stone -- Ye have gone the long way to bless them - and they have not known thee - nor are they of a mind to recognize thee ---

I say they shall be as ones awakened unto the Father's work - and they shall be as ones come alive -- I say they shall awaken and they shall come alive - I say they which have my hand upon them shall awaken -- I am not so foolish as to awaken them aforehand - for it is not lawful -

They should be as the moth which goes into the flame - they should be as the cocoon which is opened aforetime - I am not unmindful of the law ---

I say - I am mindful of my sheep - and one which is qualified to do the Father's will - thru me it is done -- So be it and Selah ---

Blest shall ye be this day - blest shall they be which come unto this altar - be they blest of me ---

I am Sananda - Son of God

Recorded by Sister Thedra of the Emerald Cross

Born - The Virgin Spirit Boran

Sori Sori Sori -- Be ye blest of me and by me -- I come unto thee from out the great cosmic heart - I bring unto thee great tidings - I bless thee with such tidings that I bring -- I say unto thee: Be ye mindful of that which I am saying unto thee at this time ---

The day is now come when one shall walk upon the Earth in flesh as Spirit made manifest - which is from out the heart of the cosmos - from out the heart of all divinity - and he shall be as God the Father incarnate in flesh -- He shall be a virgin spirit - for he has not taken upon himself a body of flesh and bone - he has not walked among man as such - he has not been as one which has gone out from the Father - he has not in any form separated himself from the Father - and he shall now go out as man - for the first time shall he go out ---

I say - he shall take upon himself the garment of flesh and bone - he shall walks as man - he shall be as man - yet he shall be as none other - for he shall be as God incarnate - he shall be as the living - breathing - pulsating life of God the Father - he shall know himself to be the Father incarnate -- And he shall go into a place which is prepared to receive him - and he shall take upon himself a body of earthly substance thru woman - I say - he shall born of the womb or woman -- He shall be the fruit of woman - yet he shall not be the seed of man - for he shall be born of God the Father - he shall be of light -- He shall be as one which has not gone into darkness - I say he shall be no part of darkness -- He shall be as one which is the perfect man - he shall be as none other -- He shall be born within the land which is called the greatest of all nations - he shall be as one filled with wisdom - and all power shall be his - for he knoweth all things -- And he has the form of man - yet he will be prepared to change it at will ---

Such shall be his knowledge. - and he shall be master of all law and all things -- I say unto thee - ye which have ears to hear and eyes to see: Be ye as ones alert and ye shall be given much which has not hitherto been revealed unto thee - lo the eons of time ye have waited ---

I say - ye have awaited this day when Earth should receive her King -- Be ye blest this day and blest shall ye be -- I am come unto thee this day that ye may be prepared for the greater part ---

I am thy Brother and thy Sibor – Boran

Recorded by Sister Thedra of the Emerald Cross

The King of Glory – "He Shall Come as A Mighty Sound – As A Mighty Trumpet"

Berean speaking unto thee: -

This day shall I speak unto thee concerning the coming of the King -- Ye have been told that the King of Glory shall make His appearance in the time which is near - it is true -- So be it ---

I come unto thee from out the cosmic center of light - I speak in all languages -- I have spoken all languages and I shall - for it is now come when many shall speak unto the Earth children -- As man shall they speak - and in the languages which each people can understand - I say each shall be spoken unto in his own language - that he may understand that which is said unto him ---

I say - we which are of the Hiarchi do speak as we do for a purpose - I say it is given in a certain manner for a purpose - and that purpose is not a mystery - for it is the greater part of wisdom -- And when ye have gone the way of the initiate it shall be revealed unto thee ---

I say - ye are an 'impatient people' filled with curiosity and wonderment -- Ye are not patient and kind - ye rush and push thy

112

way into the halls of learning - ye try to absorb thy knowledge from books - ye search the scripts and ye look for signs and for confirmation -- Ye look for peace and security - ye find none! Ye are as ones which have been following man -- Ye seek after signs and miracles - ye are as little children chasing bubbles -- I say ye shall now grow to the age of maturity - and ye shall be given as ye are prepared to receive -- I say ye shall engrave upon thy heart that which is said unto thee - and ye shall remember it - for in the days ahead all things shall pass away - and all thy knowledge of these things swept with them - ye have nothing! ye have no thing! and thy security is as naught -- I speak as one which sees and knows - I know for I am one with the Father which has given unto me being - and He has not withheld His wisdom from me -- I say ye shall stand shorn of all thy credentials - of all thy passports - of all thy glory of all thy wealth which ye have clung to so tenaciously ▪ - Ye shall stand naked - ye shall stand naked!

Ye shall be as ones wealthy indeed which do enrich thy own life with that which we bring -- I say ye shall be as ones rich indeed when ye make of thyself "A Son of God" - ye shall walk as a Son of God the Father - ye shall walk upright - ye shall give of thyself that others might be comforted - ye shall be a lamp unto their feet -- Ye shall heed these my words - mark them well - and engrave them upon thy heart - and they shall not depart from thee -----

I say ye shall listen for the trumpet which shall ring out - it shall sound thruout all the Cosmos - and ye shall awaken as from the dead -- Ye shall lift up thy eyes - and ye shall behold the King of Glory - for He shall come in as a mighty sound - as a mighty trumpet - He shall come as a great Light -- He shall come as a Mighty Host - for He shall be as one which has not been seen - - He shall be seen!

And they which are not prepared for this day shall fall upon their face and call out - Lord! Lord! - they shall freeze in their tracks from fright - they shall die of heart failure - they shall run unto a hiding place - they shall panic! And I say unto thee - they shall be as ones gone mad ---

Ye shall be as ones prepared for this day - for it is not afar off -- It has been said that the Anti Christ is now upon Earth in flesh and bone -- It is so - so be it!

We sleepeth not - nor are we unmindful of our children - we are as parents - watchful of the little ones -- We do not tarry with the trivialities - We are about the Father's business -- Such is wisdom - --

I speak unto thee from out the center of the Cosmos that ye may have Light -- I shall speak unto thee again and again -- Be ye blest of use and by me ---

I am Berean

Recorded by Sister Thedra of the Emerald Cross

Moroni Speaks

-- Be ye as Mine hand made manifest, and do that which I do, for I am One Sent that this be accomplished in the time which is <u>now</u> come - the time at hand. At no time am I to be as one which would impose upon thy free will, yet We shall do this work as ONE - of one mind, and in harmony - for in no other manner can I give unto thee the Word which I have for this people, unto which I shall speak.

Be ye as one of these people, and ye shall better understand that which I give unto them. It is now come when there shall be many changes thruout the lands of the Earth, and the inhabitants thereof shall see these changes and feel the impact thereof. So be it that there are none which shall remain untouched by such changes, for they shall be for the GOOD of all mankind; and the Work which We do shall be of Great Value unto them. Let them which have a mind to comprehend, see and know that there is help / assistance in the time of need; for this do We draw near, that they might know - that they might be as ones better prepared for that which they shall face.

Let it be known that I, Moroni, a Son of God, hast spoken out that they might have assistance; for it is now come when a NEW thing shall be done, and little are they prepared, - little are they prepared I say! for they have not done that which wast given unto them to do; they have strayed afar - followed the way of the dragon; and in this way they have errored. I say they have errored, and they have lost "The Pearl of Great Price" they have not held unto it as a precious heritage. It hast been hidden up from them, for they have misused the Gift given unto them as a Precious Jewel, to be cared for and multiplied.

Let it be said unto them that they are now as ones impoverished and alone in a strange and deserted (like unto a desert) land; for it is taken from them that which they had, - they have lost that which they had for their disobedience and insolence; their unfaithfulness hast been remembered, and it shall be accounted for.

Now, wherein hast it been said that: "They shall put their hand into the till, and they shall be as traitors, and they shall ridicule and persecute the Servants of the Living God." While they shall deny Me and the Words which I speak into thee for them, they shall be held accountable for them. They shall take thot, and be mindful of My Words, for it is now come when they shall arise and shake the dust from their garments, and put on the shining garments of Truth, and then We shall see their Light and be unto them the Friend and Helper in the time of need. We shall assist them in their effort to shake off the dust of transgression, and put on the Garment of Truth which is without blemish.

This I would say unto them: "Sit not in judgment of them which do the will of the Father," for they know not that the Father hast planned that His Servants be put to His Work; that they be served that they be brot out of bondage. So let them heed this Word, and they shall profit thereby.

Ye shall give unto them the Word which the Beloved Brother hast prepared for them, and they shall be forewarned of that which shall come upon them. They shall be caught unaware when they are as ones which think themself wise; so let them humble themself, to listen and heed the Word given unto them for their own sake.

Recorded by Sister Thedra

July 22, 1973

Awaken All Ye Which Sleepeth!!

Sori Sori -- Be ye as the hand of Me and record Mine Words which I give unto thee for them which have not received Me unto themself.

This I would say unto them: "Be ye as one prepared, for it is now come when mighty changes shall take place - and for this do I again cry unto thee: 'ARISE! AWAKEN! and hear Mine Voice' - come in and be ye as one with Me; fear not that which ye know not - that which would be unto thee thine security, thine friend and protection."

I am come that ye be delivered from harm. Wait not for signs and wonders, for thou hast had signs aplenty; wonders have I made manifest before thee, yet ye hast not read aright these manifestations, these "Signs".

I have bestowed upon thee great sights, and thou hast put thine head under thy pillow that ye see not. I have put within thy reach the Word which would be thine salvation, would ye but accept it, - ye have rejected it, and turned from them which I have sent in the name of Mine Father.

So be it that I have come as a "thief in the night" while thou hast slept. It is given unto Me to see and know thine sleep - thine lethargy hast been pitiful indeed. Thine legirons has chafed thine ankles and thou hast clung unto them as though they were thine god-given gifts.

I say unto thee: "Cut them loose - arise, seek ye thine freedom within the Light which I AM!"

Put thine hand in Mine and fear not that I shall mislead thee - I say: "PROVE ME!"

Let it be known that I have sounded the cry! The trumpet is sounded; Hear ye the cry, and heed ye the CALL; for it shall be given! But the time allotted unto man is short, and then the GREAT SILENCE! I say: Man is allotted time, and then time shall be no more. It is time to shuffle off thine lethargy, and arise and be alert unto that which goes on about thee. Pray for sight which shall be unto thee the sight of Spirit. Let thine eyes be open and thine ears shall be made to hear that which I say unto thee.

Awaken all ye which sleepeth, for I am come even as thou art, and thou seest not that which I do - thou hearest not that which I say - pity, pity is thy plight.

I am come that ye awaken. Where shall ye go? Where shall ye hide from Me? Do I not see and know where thou art, and where to find thee!? Yet how can I touch thee, when thou runneth after strange and false gods which would mislead thee, and drag thee down to perdition? Yea, I say unto thee: Thou hast followed strange gods unto the edge of the pit!

Now I say: "HALT!! go no further" for therein awaits one which would not free or deliver thee up. Why follow ye the traitor, when I am come that ye be delivered out of bondage for all time to come?

Be ye as one which hast heard and awakened - alert thyself; fail not! fall not! and know ye that I hear thy call, and I am not deceived by thine unworthy petitions - thine deceit. I am not a foolish God; I am sent of Mine Father that ye perish not!!!

So be it I am He which is Sent unto thee that ye might return unto Him - and so be it I come unto thee in His Name.

Recorded by Sister Thedra

Aug. 8, 1973

Know Peace

Sori Sori -- For this hour let it be understood that there is much to do before they know Peace, for Peace cones not from their Councils; their meetings shall fail to bring the peace which evades their efforts, for they seek not PEACE - they seek power unto themself, each in his own way. They which cry for peace have not peace, for they ask for compromise, giving not of themself in PEACE.

The peace which they find shall be but the cessation of arms for a time; yet no peace shall come unto the lands of the Earth until they cleanse themself from all hatred, greed and malice, for within themself shall peace first be established.

Look not to any man for Peace; let it be born within thine own heart - therein is the beginning and the end. Let no man take from thee thy peace, for unto each it is given - he has but to accept it as his heritage. PEACE is the LOVE OF GOD which shall first be established within each and every man.

The PEACE which I bring is within every man's reach - I say, Each and every man can attain such PEACE as I know, when he has accepted the fellowman, as I have accepted him - for the LIGHT of The WORD hast been given unto each, that he might abide upon the Earth with all other of his species.

119

The way is now open unto him, that he might come to know the plan for which he came into the world of form; form he hast, life he hast, yet he knows not his Source, neither his end - his destination. He wanders aimlessly, and for the most part arrogantly; he thinks of himself as wise, condemning all others unlike himself. For that does he falter and stumble, for none are like unto the other; for that reason do they take upon themself the responsibility of "self", that they might be as The Father would have them be. They go out as One in HIM, from HIM, and of HIM, yet separate from each other individually; that they be as "ONE" in the species of man, yet they are different in word and deed.

The WORD hast given unto each that cometh into the world a talisman that he carries with him, which no other can know, until his days upon Earth are finished; then they shall see and know even as I know, for all the masks shall at last be given up, and be of no more account - they shall be NO MORE!

There shall be a coming together as "ONE" in whose company I shall stand and speak the Word, "PASS YE, FOR THOU HAST OVERCOME".

I say: The one which overcomes flesh shall be as a FREE SOUL; no longer bound in flesh, he shall run and weary not! He shall leap for joy and fall not! He shall sing a glad anthem, and know that joy which shall be as the Hosts', for The HOST shall take up the anthem, and it shall ring thru the Cosmos, praising the Name of SOLEN AUM SOLEN.

Recorded by Sister Thedra

Now I Come Declaring

Sori Sori -- by Mine Grace shall ye be given that which shall profit thee -- ye shall first seek the LIGHT and ye shall not be deceived. Ye shall be as one responsible for the Word which is given unto thee thru this Mine handmaiden, for she hast proven herself trustworthy -- and I find her trustworthy in all things.

Be ye aware of Mine Word which is given unto thee thru and by this manner for it is good and I have declared it so -- so be it. Let thine tongue be swift to bear witness of Me, Mine Word and Mine servant for I have claimed the Word, the Work perfect, so be it and Selah. I say ye shall find no fault with the method in which it is given, for it is given in such a manner that it shall profit thee to accept it.

I say: HOLY IS THE WORD -- and I declare it so!

Be ye blest to receive it, for this I give it unto thee.

NOW I come declaring unto thee this day, that I have raised up one which I have given the power and the authority to speak for me -- I have given her Mine name that ye might have the knowledge which hast been kept for this day -- while I say there shall come ones declaring that they are mine anointed ones with the authority to speak Mine words -- I say that I know who is who -- and what is what. I say many are called and few are chosen -- this one I have called -- this one I have chosen. I have chosen her for her capacity to learn of Me -- I have chosen her for her desire to follow Me. I have chosen her for her willingness to follow Me -- there is not any deceit within her -- there is no envy or malice within her -- yet, I say into her: "COME UP HIGHER FOR I HAVE GREATER THINGS IN STORE FOR THEE". She goes where sent and comes when called.

I have placed upon her head Mine hand and I have blest her, and she hast responded unto Mine touch -- she hast rested not on her laurels. She hast wasted not her talent which I have given unto her at the altar of the Lord thy God.

I say unto thee: hear ye Me and ye shall NOT put words into Mine mouth -- neither shall ye pilfer Mine words. Ye shall not deny Mine servant -- for to deny her is to deny Me. So be it I see them cry out against Mine servant while they claim to be following Me! I say unto them: "THOU HAST NOT SEEN ME, NEITHER HEARD ME". I am come that they might know the true from the false, so let them see the LIGHT which I AM, and I say unto thee: I shall shew Mineself unto them which do seek the Light and come unto me as a little child, clean of hand and heart.

Put thine hand in mine and I shall lead thee. Come and we shall walk together and rejoice for our communication, so be it as the Father would have it. Amen and Amen.

Recorded by Sister Thedra

March 8, 1974

Forewarning
April 24, 1974

Sori Sori -- For this day let Us consider the time which is upon us
(now come). It is for this that We, the Mighty Council find it
expedient to speak unto thee, as thine Sibors, Counselors and
Brothers, I say, the time is now come, when there shall be great
upheaval, and great commotion - for the Earth too is going thru great
changes, which shall bring much devastation and sorrow. Many
shall go into the unknown realms unprepared, and they shall be
confused, and sorrow shall fill them; I say, they shall sorrow, for
they shall be as the ones unprepared.

Now the time is upon them, when they shall be brot out of the
places wherein they have labored for bread, and they shall be as ones
which have no hands - no feet with which to labor; they shall talk
without sound, for they shall be as ones without physical tongue.

They shall speak, yet no sound shall be heard; they shall cry
without tears - pity are they which go out unprepared. For this do
We say: "Pay ye heed unto that which is said unto thee" - We speak
that ye be prepared. Forget not that which is said, for We are not
given unto idle speaking. Listen, O ye people! for it is for thy sake
that We speak unto thee! So let it profit them to hear what is said.

April 24, 1974

Sori Sori -- Blest are they which come unto this Altar; Blest are they
which hear that which I say; Blest are they which accept the Word,
for I shall bless them as they have not been blest. Let them come -
let them go - and they shall find that I am the One responsible for

the Word which I give unto thee for them. Put thine hand in Mine, and I shall lead thee all the way. So be it ye shall not fail.

April 25, 1974

Sori Sori -- Place thine hand in Mine and I shall lead thee into greater heights, greater glories, and greater joys - so be it Amen.

May 1, 1974

Sori Sori -- For this day, let Us be as the Ones Sent that they might know that there are Ones which KNOW from whence they come, and whereto they shall go. And let them learn that there are ones which have taken upon themself flesh and bone - born of woman - which still sleep - yet to awaken. And these We, of the "Host" are to find and awaken; it is for their sake that We come into the Earth at this time. It is said, "They" shall awaken, and know that they have slept - slept overtime. Now they shall be found and awaken, and come forth as ones prepared to go all the way with Me the Lord thy God - so let it be and Selah.

Recorded by Sister Thedra

Sanat Kumara speaking:-

I shall say: My hand be upon thee, and I shall cause thee to be quickened of tongue and spirit, and ye shall be as one blest of Me - for is it not said, that one shall hear Me and receive what I have to offer? I say, yea, even more than one shall receive that which I have received, for I will give unto those prepared, as I have been given, and unto them shall be given a part - their part. Each has a part - therefore, step forth and take that which is thy responsibility. Come

124

unto thy own altar with an empty cup, to proffer thy Father; ask of Him to send the Heavenly Teachers, that ye may be lead rightly. Thou will be prepared, and I say: Trust in the Lord thy God, for it is so.

Let not thy heart be troubled, for He shall give unto thee strength, and ye shall fear not.

I say: Arise, all who sleepeth, and begin thy real work.

That is My word unto men at this time. That is all -

I AM Sanat Kumara

Maroni: -

I say: I too would speak unto men, for I shall soon draw nigh unto the many who have awakened. I say, Oh men: Prepare thyself as an empty vessel, that I may come into thee and fill thy cup. I say: If thy cup is full, where shall I pour My new drink - the Water of Life? I say: Do ye prefer thy intoxicating elixir, to the wine of Bliss?

Let ye not be slow on thine feet, for I shall come, and I shall go, and thou shalt be unaware of Mine presence, lest thou art prepared. So do I say: Awaken thyselves - I will draw close to those aware; I will give unto them of the Heavenly Ways, for I shall not be as one of their frivolous manners. I know why I come - I do not waver in My Work; I say, I know! I know fully!

That is My Message this day. Let all who hear, hear/ see, see.

I Am Maroni

They Shall Awaken

Sori Sori;- Give forth unto them as I would ye do. I say that there are many who are ready to awaken unto their part, for the decree has gone out, and it is a mighty one. The call to awaken has been sounded from top of the Mount, and I say: Hear ye, who would have an understanding of My Words.

As ye have prepared yourselves, so shall ye receive of My Grace/ My Presence. I say: I shall cause many to step forth, for they shall awaken unto their true purpose, and they shall be about the Father's business. Many shall come forth, prepared to do as instructed, for I shall cause them to do so.

Not one, but many shall there be who are of My fold. The flock shall grow in number and multiply greatly. I shall cause this to be, for it is part of the Plan.

I say unto all who do hear this My Word: Blest shall ye be for thy forbearance and preservation in thy holy ways. I am with thee, and there is great strength at thy side.

Be in peace - a servant of thy Father's Will/Plan. Do not hesitate to believe strongly - I say: Have faith in thy Source, and in the Lord God. Love ye one another as I have loved you. That is My word unto men this day.

I AM Sananda

Feign Not Deafness

Sanat Kumara speaking: -

Know that the hand of God is upon the Earth - the time moves swiftly, and I bid ye wait no more. Awaken unto thy being - unto thy Source, unto thy part. The flock shall multiply, and yet is it given thee that ye shall be of one mind/one purpose. Ye shall be single of eye; ye shall know what ye are about, and ye shall do your work in the world, by the sustenance of the hand of God.

Hear Us, My peoples - feign not deafness. The call has gone forth: It is now time to be up and about the more important things of thy life.

Listen well in thy times of silence and meditations - We are with thee.

I AM Sanat Kumara

Prepare Thyselves Well

Now record as I would have ye, for the good of thine brethren: The time approaches; many shall be the ones who shall meet face to face with Self - I say: Therein is the judgment - the reckoning; therein is the time whence ye shall see the folly of flesh, and the bewilderment of the mind. Through the veil ye shall gaze at thy Earth; thy Life; and ye shall wonder greatly at its vagary.

I say: Many shall there be, who will pass from the Earth Realm - and I warn: "Prepare thyselves well" - prepare that ye may be ready to go to the place which will take you in - for not all will go to the same place.

And I say: Trust not unto man, for he too is in darkness. Trust only upon the Light, for therein is Wisdom. I say: Call ye upon the

Light of God, and ye shall be taken care of. Follow not in the current stream with thy brothers, for they rush unaware into places they know not of. Awaken now - be alert; the time of reckoning draws nigh unto thee.

Therefore do I say: "Call on thy Lord God, the Host - ask of thy Source for guidance unto higher Truth - wait not! wait not!"

That is My Word -

I AM Sananda

Ye Would Profit Best to Wait No More

Sanat Kumara speaking; -

This day ye shall record thusly: It is nigh the time when many shall be sobered, either by choice, or by circumstance. Happy shall be the ones who have chosen of their own free will, for therein is Wisdom. Blessed are those who have believed without proof, for their faith shall be their salvation.

Now I say unto the many: Stand not back; come forth; Learn and prepare for what is ahead of thee. It is no small task, and ye would profit best to wait no more. The hand of God moves swiftly, and I shall say: The end time draws nigh for many. Yet shall ye be aware of the many factors of the Dragon/the Black Hood, for therein lies the key to thy suffering. It is of thy own creation, and ye shall feign not thy unknowing. Be alert unto thy times - there is stress and there is chaos at hand. Waste not thy time; call now upon thy Source; reckon with thy self; transmute thy misused energy - I say: Ye shalt, or ye shall be sorrowful.

I have spoken that ye may have Light. I am not One to fool, nor be fooled; I come forth with the Power of God Almighty, to give unto thee warning.

These are My Words, Blest are they who see the Light, and believe therein.

I AM Sanat Kumara

They Shall Be Willing to Serve

Sananda speaking; -

I shall say this: Many are the ones who are prepared to accept their own responsibility, and play a part in the Plan. The workers are of many domains, and plentiful are the parts to be filled. I shall raise up those who do show themself willing, for I shall find them by their Light. By their light they shall be known, for therein lies the truth of their being.

Now the ones which I shall raise up shall prepare for their part, and they shall go about it knowingly and with joy. And they shall be as a willing servant, and I shall give unto them as they are prepared to receive.

Let Me say too: They shall be willing to serve in any capacity; to go and come when called. The times at hand shall require many of strength and forbearance - and yet I do say: I am thy strength and forbearance; I am thy Shield and thy Buckler. Let all who would, place their hand in Mine, and by thy faith ye shall be led into the Greater Part. Be at Peace -

I AM Sananda

There Is a Part for Each

Sori Sori -- Let each claim that which is rightfully his, for the Father has willed unto each and every one their Divine Sonship. I say: "Arise, O man - know thyself to be that which ye truly are". There are none so foolish as those which think themselves wise. Ye have laid up thy wisdom in the material world, and ye have forgotten the spiritual. I say: With all thy fancy schools and degrees, ye have missed the true Essence of Life. I say: "Awaken now - let go of all thine opinions and ideas; empty thy cup, and call unto Me. Present thyself as an empty vessel, that I may pour out My Spirit unto thee".

I say: Go into thy secret chambers, and there make right those things which doth cause you discomfort. I say: Go unto thy neighbor, and if thou dost hold a grudge against him, make thy slate clean - then I say: Come unto Me - come as a child, with no expectancies, other than the ecstasy of the moment; come as one willing; as one open; come as one willing to serve thine brethren in any capacity. "Come! Come! Come!" that is My Call, for I shall see that all who do heed it, and come with an open and sincere heart, are given a part. There is a part for each; there is a special part for each, according to their individual preparation. I have said many times: "As ye are prepared, so shall ye receive".

I say: Take My Word, and spread it among man, that he may know I have returned. The Lord God is here. And I have come to gather unto Me Mine own - My flock. And I say: Mine know Me, and I know Mine own. I ask ye, dear reader - are ye of My flock?

Heed well the Words contained herein, for thou shalt be cautioned against denial of them. If ye do deny My Word, ye do deny Me.

Again I say: "Come unto Me!

I AM thy Lord God, Sananda

US thine Ambassadors of Peace and Goodwill. I say, place thine hand in Ours, and We shall reveal Ourself as Brothers, true, and strong - thine Benefactors which thou hast spurned in past days - years - yea for long hast <u>thou</u> turned away as frightened children.

I say, be ye not afrighted, for We come bringing glad tidings unto all - yet it is given unto Us to see thee running as the animal chased by the hound.

I say, we come that ye be lifted up - that ye might have greater knowledge of thine Source of being; of thine place of abode; of the place wherein ye shall go when thine time is finished within thine present place of abode. It is said thine days are numbered, and rightly so, for We see and know as thou knowest not that which We are prepared to reveal unto thee. We see clearly - thou "Seest as thru the glass darkly". I say, We come that there be no mystery. While ye make mystery, We come to make things clear unto all.

Now it is said: "Fear not" - I ask, why fear? why fear for thine life - when We are come that ye might understand thine life, and that ye have life more abundantly? Why grovel ye in the pit? I have watched thee grovel for a pittance, while We thine Benefactors offer thee an abundance of greater things than thou hast imaged.

Be as one prepared to receive Us of the Higher Realms, and we shall reward thee openly.

I am one which hast revealed Mineself unto this one which hast volunteered to be Mine hand made manifest unto the unknowing ones - which await the greater revelations. So be it that I shall speak again and ye shall remember that I have spoken.

Remember Me, for I shall speak unto thee as ...

Recorded by Sister Thedra

Why Fear - Thy Benefactors

Sori Sori -- Mine hand I place upon thine head in holy benediction, and I say unto thee, I am thine Shield and thy Buckler - I have given unto thee a part separate from all others, and I have cared for thee that ye be as one prepared for the Greater part. Now ye shall be blest to receive of Me a New Part, which shall be given unto them which hast gone thus far with thee. Now ye shall bless them by the Word which ye shall receive for them, which have a mind to receive. So let them be blest of Me thru thee - I am come that they be blest.

They shall receive these Mine Words thru thee, for by thine Grace shall they receive. It is for their sake that I say unto thee, arise and get thineself prepared to give unto them these words. Thou hast heard and obeyed - therefore I say unto them, they shall be blest thru thee, by Me - so may it be.

Now ye shall give unto them the Word that I am prepared to give unto thee for them. It is Mine part to give unto thee the WORD - thine part to receive it, prepare it for them, and present it unto them - let them accept it or deny it as they will. While the hour swiftly approaches when they shall stand before the throne of Justice, they shall do well to listen unto that which I say unto them. There are now many which cry out for relief from their afflictions which doth beget them - yet they seek man's blessing and his advice - while I say: "Come unto Me and I shall show unto thee many things which shall be new and strange" - which shall cause thine heart to rejoice. And thine time shall no more be consumed by trifles or small things, for I say, I know that which ye have not known - ye have not yet dreamed of such wonders as I might shew unto thee - for this have I said, be ye as ones prepared for greater things. The trifles shall no longer entice thee, after ye have glimpsed the greatness of the things which I am now prepared to shew thee; thine mind hast not conceived of such wonders!

Ye shall be as ones filled with wonder and joy for thine knowing.

Yet ye shall be as ones silent, and give not thine pearls of great price into the unknowing ones. While much hast been revealed unto them, they for the most part know not that which hast been revealed - they know not how to read the "Signs of The Times". The day hast come when We draw nigh unto the Earth that all might come to know the Truth! It is said: "Seek the Truth and it shall free thee of all bondage", it is so - so let it be as ye are prepared to receive. Now it is come when they shall see, and doubt their eyes - yea their sanity, for I say they shall stand in awe and wonderment; they shall flee for fear, and cry for peace; they shall pray for help, knowing not that

HELP IS COME - I say: HELP IS COME! why art thou not mindful of it - Us thine Benefactors!!

Pick up thine feet; step forth; put out thine hand and receive.

The Light Must Be Anchored

-- I say unto thee, that thou shalt do what has been given, for I have touched thee, and ye shall be quickened even more. Many shall know My touch, for the times ahead demand that the many are awake unto that which must be done. The Light must be anchored; the Light must be centered. It is now greater than ever before - for a decree has gone out of the mouth of the Mighty Father, to "Bring them home". Yet I say: "Only those prepared can receive their Sonship". The Father would have all - but the Law is the Law.

Now too I say: This country is in great need. The workers are necessary - workers for the Light. Each one who is willing to serve in any capacity: step forth and prove thyself trustworthy; as ye do show thyself true unto the lesser - more shall be added unto thee.

Too, the workers which come forth and declare unto Me: "Here I am Lord, take me into Thy Service", shall come clean of hand, empty of cup - they shall come as ones empty of all opinions and creeds - those things shall be left behind. And too I say: These workers shall be pure of heart, and single of eye. They shall offer hands, hearts, will, unto their Source - and this is the better part.

Think, dear reader, that thou art of this great Call? I say: All who are willing are called. Come unto me in the silence of thy own temple, and offer to Me thy being, that it may be used for the good of all, Be ye at Peace -

I AM Sananda

Be Ready and Prepare

Give forth unto all men, that which I would say at this time. Thy planet is at the verge of great change; there IS much confusion, much bewilderment approaching. The Elements shall turn tail, and tolerate no more thy wonton ways - they shall heap destruction upon thy places of habitat, and there will be much sadness. It is the Law that: "As ye sow ye do reap". Therefore, it is only the reaping of thy own actions, and can be blamed on none other but self.

My Call has gone out; the need is for those strong of faith, strong of heart. I need those who will meet the trials and tribulations of the coming time, on their feet - who will remain on solid ground and not waver before the great test - for these shall be as the Light for all the areas of the world; and these shall be as the comforters unto the many in darkness, who understand not what is happening.

These who do answer My Call, shall be as ones willing, and waiting My directions; they will be as ones glad for their part, in service to Our Father's Great Plan.

I feign not that the way is easy; I have said over and over again: "The path is narrow and steep". But I am the Rock on which this Temple is built; I AM the Rock upon all who do serve My Father shall lean; I AM the Sure Foundation - I waver not, for I KNOW - I KNOW!!

Give forth, then, thy hands, heart, will, unto thy calling. Be ready and prepare well for what is to come. I say: "Be ready and PREPARE!!"

I AM Sanat Kumara

Arise All Ye Who Sleepeth

Be ye as My Hand made manifest, and say unto them, that the time is at hand. Wait no longer to decide which way ye shall go. Shall ye continue to serve the Dragon, it is a sad lot indeed. Turn thine eyes upward unto thy Lord God, for therein shall be thy deliverance. It is by My Hand and the power invested Me from the Most High Father, Solen Aum Solen, that ye are able now to overstep the bounds of the Earth plane. It is time for many to rise from their sleep - awaken and be about that for whence they came. And these shall be the lucky ones - for they have fortuned unto themself the strength to awaken, and have done so with My assistance, for they are as the ones who know Me to be with them.

Arise all ye who sleepeth - arise I say, put on the whole Armor of God, for your tine has come. I say: Your time has arrived; if it were not so, I would say not.

Be not foolish; be ye not among the laggards, who wait with their thumbs in their mouth - these shall be as the sad ones - they shall wait too long, and therein shall be the sadness.

Come unto Me now, in the stillness of thy heart, with Love and willingness of spirit, that I may touch thee, and depart unto thee My Peace and My Will.

Arise I say - Sleep no more.

I AM thy Lord God Sananda

www.ingramcontent.com/pod-product-compliance
Lightning Source LLC
Chambersburg PA
CBHW070810050426
42452CB00011B/1973